Three Muslims & a Jew

Morris Aaron Shapiro

TRILOGY CHRISTIAN PUBLISHERS

TUSTIN, CA

Trilogy Christian Publishers
A Wholly Owned Subsidary of Trinity Broadcasting Network
2442 Michelle Drive
Tustin, CA 92780

For information, address Trilogy Christian Publishing

Rights Department, 2442 Michelle Drive, Tustin, CA 92780.

Trilogy Christian Publishing/ TBN and colophon are trademarks of Trinity Broadcasting Network.

For information about special discounts for bulk purchases, please contact Trilogy Christian Publishing.

Manufactured in the United States of America

Trilogy Disclaimer: The views and content expressed in this book are those of the author and may not necessarily reflect the views and doctrine of Trilogy Christian Publishing or the Trinity Broadcasting Network.

10 9 8 7 6 5 4 3 2 1

Library of Congress Cataloging-in-Publication Data is available.

ISBN 978-1-64773-148-9

ISBN 978-1-64773-149-6

Contents

Foreword

I feel like I've always known my brother and friend Morey. We shared so many childhood memories, from playing sports, having to attend Hebrew school, trading baseball cards to attending birthday parties. Even at a young age, I could sense Morey was a gentle soul. He was one of the few kids in our gang, who never judged others. I believe God puts people in our lives to teach us things we need to learn. Morey taught me tolerance and goodwill. In this book, Morey takes his readers on an insightful journey. We get to see Morey's development from childhood to manhood and then his quest to become a whole human being. His faith is tested many times on this straight and narrow road. But as all true heroes realize, those who persevere with devout conviction will find the inner joy and peace they have long searched for. We live in an age where division and prejudice seem to be the norm. This story serves to expose the fundamental oneness of humanity. Morey has the courage and tenacity to shine the light of truth in a world of darkness.

—Alan Siegel, Writer, classmate, friend

Introduction

I come from a family of storytellers. Whenever I get together with my brother and sisters, we always reminisce about our crazy, childhood adventures. When I was young, it was all about fun and games. As I grew older, life took on a whole new meaning, and these stories reflect both the victory and tragedy of my experience. All of the events recorded in this book are true, but most of the names have been changed to protect the innocent, namely me. I hope you will relate to both the laughter and the heartache of my journey as well as to the tales of many of the people I've met on life's winding road.

God bless you all,

Morey

CHAPTER ONE

The Three Muslims

It was a warm Sunday afternoon in May when I received a phone call that would change the course of my summer. My son's tennis partner had canceled, and he was looking for a replacement. My wife, Carol, and I both love the sport, so we decided to rally with him. Shortly after we started playing, we were approached by a man with a dark complexion and jet-black hair who spoke with a foreign accent. He wanted to join us and make a foursome for a doubles match. We quickly agreed.

"What country are you from?" I queried.

"Guess!" he responded.

"Egypt?" I attempted.

"I'm from Turkey," he corrected.

He was a pretty decent player, and we had a good time on the court. Afterward, we thought we should invite him to our house for refreshments. He seemed delighted and asked if his two friends could come along.

"Sure," I replied.

The whole plan seemed innocent enough. We settled into chairs and made some small talk. Then Carol dropped the bomb.

"What religion are you?"

"We're Muslims," they proudly proclaimed. She couldn't stop there!

"My husband loves to talk about religion!" she shot back.

I wanted to crawl under the couch at that point since Muslims and Jews have been known not to get along!

But her remark seemed to be the invitation they were waiting for since, in their culture, there's no reservation in discussing either religion or politics. In fact, for the next three hours, there was shouting and much emotional outburst, which they seemed to relish as we discussed the Bible and the Koran.

The three Muslims who called themselves Mike, Mel, and Nick (having adopted English names to try to assimilate to American culture) seemed to have one simple philosophy regarding religion. "You are what you're born," they kept insisting. But this was not true for me—not anymore.

Well, maybe I should start at the beginning. My story began long before I was born in a land far to the north.

MORRIS AARON SHAPIRO

CHAPTER TWO

A Unique Heritage

My mother, Hilda Gummer, was a lovely, young woman, fair-skinned and freckled with beautiful strawberry blonde hair and sparkling blue eyes, which gleamed with a mischievous air. Just seventeen, she felt very grown up now that she'd landed a job at the glove factory in Toronto and moved away from home. She had been eager to leave the farm where she'd been raised to see what the big world was all about. She'd been quite sheltered, as were most young girls of that era. It had been quite a stable, peaceful life on the family farm where they raised sheep and cattle and grew their own vegetables. She was a country girl from Prescott in Ontario.

Hilda was athletic and energetic as well as a real extravert, who loved to laugh and even pull a prank now and then. And, of course, like virtually every young woman of her day, her main goal in life was to find a husband, get married, and have a family. There was no time to lose in achieving that dream either. Girls who waited too long might risk becoming old maids like her cousin who'd just turned twenty-six and had no prospects.

So, when not-so-tall but debonair, dark, and handsome Harry Shapiro appeared on the job one day, she was up for the challenge.

"Ooh, he's nice-looking!" she whispered to her coworker.

"I bet you can't get him to ask you on a date," her friend jibed.

"I bet I can," Hilda retorted.

With Hilda's natural charm and winning smile, he did ask, several times, in fact. She wasn't sure at first if she should accept. He was, after all, an older man fully seven years her senior. And there was something else; something she knew very little or nothing about that she'd heard whispered around the shop: "He's Jewish!" She'd never met a Jew before and couldn't remember ever seeing any in her small town of a few thousand people. *But why should a person's religion make a difference?* she thought. *This was 1938, not the dark ages!*

From their first date at the soda fountain, as she chattered happily if somewhat nervously and he smiled and listened politely, they were swept up in a strong current of romance and destiny. After they'd courted about two months, Harry knew it was time to propose. No one needed to tell him this. This was just how things were done in that day. Men weren't afraid to make that swift decision back then. In fact, it was expected of them. He also knew that it was time to talk to his parents.

"So, she's a nice Jewish girl, right? Where does her family go to temple? What! She's not Jewish!"

His mother, who'd been pouring coffee, now desperately needed a chair.

"Son, what were you thinking? How could you do this?" his father shouted in an uncharacteristically loud tone.

His father wasn't just any Jewish man, either. This was Morris Aaron Shapiro, son of the high priest. The original family name of Jourard had been lost in the immigration process when he and several siblings had come to Canada from Lithuania. His father was a Frenchman who married a Lithuanian woman and moved to her country.

Harry was dumbfounded. The truth was he hadn't given the relationship a lot of thought from the religious perspective. Any misgivings, he'd had, he'd quickly brushed aside as he'd gazed at Hilda's striking face and figure.

"But I love her!" he stammered. "She's beautiful!"

"The son of the high priest can't marry a gentile! What would your children be?" His father's face was now several shades redder.

His mother choked back sobs. And listening in the other room, his older sister fumed, subconsciously vowing to hate this gentile hussy who'd seduced her baby brother.

There was an extremely long silence. But Harry wasn't backing down. It was too late for that!

"Son, you know there's only one way," his father finally intoned.

❖

"You mean you want me to change my religion?" Hilda exclaimed in shock to Harry's much more subtle and subdued statement.

This was obviously not on her to-do list of wedding preparations.

"You mean they won't accept me if I'm not Jewish!" she blurted out furiously.

He hadn't seen her in anger before. He wished he didn't have to ask this. He'd never wanted to hurt her or anyone for that matter!

How much did she love him? How far should she have to go to please her man? Or his family? It really seemed to be too much! Hilda's heart was overwhelmed with conflicting emotions.

Actually, she had never found her religion to be so terribly important to her. Like almost every respectable family of the day, the Gummer's had attended church services. Hilda had gone to Sunday School and learned the basic tenets of the Christian faith at their Anglican parish. This was expected of all the community there, but it had never held any great excitement for her. To her, religion was a formality, a set of rules and rituals that had their place, but it was definitely not the focal point of her life. She was more into sports—like ice skating in the winter and swimming in summer. She swam across the St. Lawrence Seaway when she was only thirteen. Still, the Anglican church was very much a part of her heritage. What right did Harry or his family have to demand that she give that up? Everything had been going so well for the two of them until this! She hadn't told her parents of the engagement yet, not exactly. She'd just given some strong hints in her last letter of an attachment that was becoming stronger by the day to a wonderful man she'd been seeing for a while now. Surely, they wouldn't take issue with him being Jewish. They were better than that! But should she, could she change her religion? What would her parents think of that? Tears welled up in her eyes. Her heart ached, and her head was spinning. She knew she had to go home. Her first real bout of homesickness suddenly hit her like a tsunami.

❖

Harry and Hilda clung to each other as she prepared to board the train. He begged her not to leave him. She promised to return, even smiled, and blew kisses from the window as the train slowly lumbered away down the tracks.

Home had never looked so appealing to Hilda, as she ran across the farmyard to greet old Shep, the English sheepdog who tended their small flock. Her father, a butcher, had cooked a roast of pork and made a special meal for her homecoming. The family circle felt so good to her, so soothing. She wanted to forget the high drama of her romance and the looming, life-changing decisions that weighed on her for a little while.

"So, Hilda, when are you going to tell us about your beau?" her mother queried with a mixture of pride and apprehension. "We thought you'd have brought him with you the way you'd spoken in your letter."

"Oh, well, what do you want to know?" Hilda laughed a tad nervously.

"His name would be a good start," her mother cracked.

"His name is Harry Shapiro," Hilda said proudly.

"Shapiro? What kind of name is that?" her father barked loudly.

Hilda had always been Daddy's girl. For as long as she could remember, she'd been his particular favorite. Nothing could change that.

She smiled confidently at him, "It's Jewish."

"Jewish! You mean you're seeing a Jew?" he growled with anger so intense it made her tremble.

"Yes, Daddy. What's wrong with that?" she questioned naively.

"What's wrong? Everything!" he raved in fury. "My daughter is not marrying any Jew!"

"No, Hilda. It wouldn't be right," her mother chimed in.

"But just wait till you meet him, Dad! You'll change your mind. He's a good man! He's polite and kind. Everyone likes him! He even has a college education."

"I will never meet him, Hilda, and you will not marry him!" he pounded his fist like a gavel on the table.

There had been an awful finality to that gesture. A verdict had been rendered, and with that verdict came the end of an era. She would never be Daddy's special, little girl again. She had a terrible choice to make, one that no woman should have to face.

"If you marry him, I'll never speak to you again!" James Gummer roared at his departing daughter as she boarded the train back to Toronto. And tragically, he never did. Hilda had made her decision, and she stood by her man as the wheels of fate kept rapidly turning.

❖

She didn't feel any different after she took her Jewish vows—more ritual and religious rites! Now, hopefully, at least one set of parents would accept her. She stuffed the overpowering weight of her parent's rejection somewhere deep inside, lest it crush her completely.

The wedding was small and very Jewish. The story goes that since none were willing to marry a Jew and Gentile, my father had to bribe a rabbi to marry them. But, thankfully, Dad's parents now seemed to accept their son's bride. His father even gave her a mink stole for a wedding gift, which was appropriate since he ran a clothing store.

There had been blessings spoken over the newly-weds for fruitfulness, but as the years slipped by, the olive branches failed to appear. This was especially grievous to Hilda, who felt the burden to produce an heir was part of her new religious duty. Did Harry seek the God of Abraham on her behalf, as did the ancient patriarchs for their barren wives? It would be surprising if he hadn't, at least after a doctor told them they could never have children. But God answers prayer, and after seven years, she did conceive. A daughter was born. Then after only a year and a half, another daughter came into their lives. Then four years passed, and a third daughter was born. The olive tree was really thriving at that point because two years later, I was born. I guess doctors make mistakes, and God does miracles. I was followed by a brother and another sister. In fact, sadly, there were also four miscarriages, and when she was pregnant with her seventh child, the doctor told her an abortion would be necessary to save her life. She, at first, refused, but he convinced her to do it since she had six children who needed her.

Looking back, I can see how the unresolved trauma, pain, anger, and rejection built up inside my mother to reach a breaking point. She confided to me that for many years after she converted to Judaism, she was rarely accepted by either Jews or Gentiles, with the exception of her in-laws. I don't think Dad's sister ever accepted her. And, worst of all, her father was killed in a car accident ten years after her marriage without there ever being any reconciliation between them. Her marriage and conversion came at an awful price.

CHAPTER THREE

Childhood Adventures

As a child, I never understood why Mommy was constantly in bed. Now I realize she was in severe depression. She gave me as much love as she could. I am told I was left in the playpen a lot, but I remember my childhood as one big, crazy adventure. As kids, my siblings and I ran wild. Mom's incapacity and Dad's work schedule left us with very little supervision. In my childish mind, of course, I had no concept of the dangers or consequences of running totally wild. I was a happy little boy.

My parents had moved to Gloversville, New York, after my sister Marsha was born, where Dad took a job in a leather mill. In the stately, well to do Jewish neighborhood we lived in, our household was notorious for complete chaos on a continuous basis. We were the neighbors they make movies about.

My earliest memory goes back to when I was just two years old. There was a sandbox in my backyard, which I loved to play in. One day I was enjoying that sandbox when suddenly, I heard a terrible scream. My sisters were playing in the yard and had scaled a high fence so that they could climb onto the garage roof.

When my sister Sharon, who was only four years old, tried to climb the fence, she fell and was seriously injured. My sisters cried for my mother, and they all took off in a frenzy to the emergency room. After they had been there for some time, my mother had the horrifying realization that I wasn't with them. She immediately called a neighbor to check on me and rushed home in a panic. To her immense relief, she found me still in the sandbox, safe and sound. I'm sure my guardian angel must have been by my side.

I remember the day my mother took me to the dentist, and when we returned, I saw a huge fire truck out front and firefighters all around the house. My sister, Marsha, had been left to babysit, and it seemed like all the kids in the neighborhood came over. They were playing hide and seek with her, and they all ran up into the attic. She thought to play a little trick on them and locked the attic door. But when she tried to unlock the door, the old skeleton key got stuck and then broke. The children were trapped, and they thought there wasn't enough oxygen, so they panicked and started breaking windows. Some of the glass from the windows landed on my youngest sister, Janet, who was in her baby carriage outside. Miraculously she was sound asleep and unharmed. Marsha called the fire department to the rescue. When Mom and I burst onto the scene, she spotted a firefighter poised with a large ax ready to break down the attic door.

"You stupid idiot, take the hinges off!" Mom screamed.

His glory bubble burst, but he heeded her wisdom. How ironic that my oldest sister, Renee, ended up marrying that firefighter's son.

Another time, my older sisters were smoking in the attic, when they heard my parents come in the front door. They quickly extinguished their cigarettes and ran downstairs like little angels. Little did they know that the cigarette ashes, which fell on a mattress, would ignite. Just as my parents were ready to go out for the evening, a neighbor called having seen big flames in the attic window. We all ran outside in a panic and were rescued by the fire department once again. These are just a few examples of the types of episodes that were continually happening at our house.

My best friend, Bobby, lived across the street from us, and it seemed like I spent most of my childhood at his house. I was the terror of the neighborhood, and his mother dreaded my arrival, as did most of the other parents. Since I'd never been taught any manners or received much discipline, I did whatever I wanted until I was confronted.

Bobby wasn't very well supervised either. We went on adventures alone when we were only six or seven years old. He was quite a devious little boy and would steal money from his mother's wallet. Then he'd lead me downtown where we would buy lots of goodies. This went on for weeks before his mother finally caught on, and then she naturally blamed me.

But Bobby wouldn't give up that easily. He was committed, even at that age, to a life of crime. So, like a junior mob boss, he then ordered me to make the next heist. He told me to raid my mother's purse.

"She won't miss only a couple of dollars," he promised.

My mother was fast asleep in her bed, so the pickings seemed easy. I can still see her bright red pocketbook perched on the dresser. I glanced once more in her direction. She was still snoozing. I quickly found her wallet and flipped it open and then prepared to follow my friend's dictates. The only problem was that all I could find was a twenty-dollar bill. I snatched it out and hurried away. Bobby was waiting. We were ready to go shopping. We hiked to the grocery store just several blocks away.

What a blast we had! We bought as many toys and treats as we could carry away. I remember I had a giant cowboy in one hand and a bag of tootsie roll pops in the other hand. We were gleefully strolling back down the street toward home when suddenly, my mother drove up to the curb beside us. She ordered us to get in the car. She then drove back to the store and made us return all the items we'd bought. She also gave the clerk a thorough tongue lashing for allowing such young boys to purchase all those goods on their own.

When we arrived home, I received the worst spanking of my life and got a huge lecture about the evils of stealing. She even threatened to call the police. I think she may have instilled a healthy fear in me at that point, which kept me from joining my friends in a shoplifting spree as a teenager. Three of my buddies were caught and charged with felonies. The scripture says, "Train up a child in the way he should go, and when he is old he will not depart from it" (Proverbs 22:6 KJV).

I can remember one of the many times I was rewarded for tattling on my sisters. It must have been a really juicy story since my mother gave me a half dollar. I was thrilled! I went over to Bobby's house, proudly flipping the coin in the air until his mother caught it and called me a thief.

I was a pretty insecure kid. I had a face full of freckles and a silver cap on one of my front teeth that I had chipped in an early boyhood scuffle. I never smiled since kids had made fun of my "silver trophy". And my mother compounded the problem when she picked out silver frames for my eyeglasses. I was the only kid in my first-grade class with glasses and a silver cap on my tooth.

My utter lack of home training was often manifested at school resulting in much negative attention from teachers. I'd gotten extremely tired of one teacher telling me to zip up my fly, so I thought I'd devised the perfect solution. The next day when the same teacher came around asking me to zip it up, I told her I didn't need to since I was wearing my swim trunks under my pants. The strategy paid off in another way later that day.

After school, I was invited home by the superintendent of school's son and stayed for dinner. My table manners were atrocious since we kids never ate with our parents. We also never had Italian meals at our house, and they were serving spaghetti. I'd seen birds eat worms, so I started slurping up the pasta. My friend's father asked me if I'd eaten spaghetti before and showed me the proper way to eat it. After dinner, my friend's parents couldn't wait to get rid of me.

His father said, "Morey, it's too bad you don't have your bathing suit with you because we're all going to the YMCA for swim night."

My face lit up, and I said, "No problem, I've got my bathing suit on, and I'd love to go with you!" Needless to say, I was never invited to that house again.

At another friend's home, I bowled an ostrich egg, which was a prized possession, laughing as it shattered into a million pieces. The mother screamed at me and told me I was no longer welcome to visit there. She also told me the egg had cost a hundred dollars, and that I would have to pay them the money. I remember afterward walking down the street with my buddy Neil, trying to calculate how long it would take me to save up enough money from my twenty-five cents a week allowance to pay them the hundred dollars. I figured it would take about eight years, and I'd be seventeen by then.

My little brother, Jeff, and I had endured a lot of torment at the hands of our older sisters, who were our usual babysitters. One night when my parents hired a friend's teenage daughter to watch us, I drew the line. They told her to make sure we took our baths, put on our pajamas, and got to bed early. We didn't like baths or pajamas, and we wanted to stay up late. So, when this naive fifteen-year-old girl tried to initiate the orders, I came up with a plan.

I told her, "Our pajamas are in the basement. Would you please bring them to us?" At first, she hesitated, but we pleaded with her, telling her we were afraid to go down in the cellar. Our cellar was a dark and scary place. We knew the light didn't work, but we told her it was at the bottom of the stairs. After she had groped her way slowly down the steps, I slammed the door and locked it. She was terrified and started screaming for us to open the door. We told her we would let her come up under three conditions: No baths, no pajamas, and no bedtime! She realized she had to meet our demands or remain our hostage. She never said another word that night, and we never saw her again. That was the last babysitter my parents ever hired.

I wasn't crazy about school, but I guess I can't say I hated all my subjects. I remember one science project that turned out to be kind of fun. Our sixth-grade teacher divided us into groups of four. Each group was to study a different topic. A boy named Charlie was the leader of my group, and he decided we should study snakes. It was an all-boy team, and this choice appealed to each one of us. Fortunately, there aren't many poisonous snakes in that part of the country.

We then went on a snake hunting adventure. We learned how to pick them up without getting bitten. I brought a cigar box along to stash our captives in. We collected a total of seven small snakes in a variety of colors. We excitedly headed back home, anxious to show off our booty.

Along the way, we stopped at the candy store since I had a dime on me. I put the box of reptiles down next to the many bins of penny candy, as I prepared to make my selections. But somehow, in my haste, I knocked the box over, and all the snakes escaped into the candy. They were slithering around happily amidst the tootsie rolls and red hots when the owner spotted them.

"Get those snakes out of here, and don't you ever come back!" he screamed at us. We quickly caught six of them and dashed out of the shop, knowing, though, that there was one more lurking in there somewhere! Someone was going to get a not so sweet surprise that day.

Since I grew up in a neighborhood with about twenty Jewish families and the children all attended the same elementary school, I didn't even notice at first that I was any different from most kids with regards to my religious faith. I do remember, though, that all the Jewish kids were separated from the rest of the class when Christmas carols were sung or pageants were performed. Our parents had demanded this.

Naturally, I was curious to know who this Jesus was and what all the hoopla was about. So, I tried to find out. I went home one day and asked my father. "Who's Jesus?"

"Don't you ever mention that name!" he commanded, shaking his finger in my face. So, I asked the rabbi, "Who is Jesus?" and received the same response. I could see hatred in his eyes. This prohibition only seemed to pique my interest.

I think it's easy for people these days to look down upon this type of religious prejudice, but at that time, the Jews had only recently come through the Holocaust. They had been labeled "Christ killers" by the Nazis, many of whom went to church on Sunday and fired up the gas chambers on Monday. It's important to understand why people think and act the way they do.

I didn't detect any racial prejudice in my parents. I do remember, however, that there was one family they didn't like. Every Sunday after the ballgame was over, my mother would prod my father to take us out for a Sunday drive. We kids were glad to go since we knew we'd get ice cream cones. Ice cream cones only cost ten cents back in the fifties. As we were driving down the highway, I often overheard my parents talking about how terrible the gentiles were. *I never wanted to meet that family*, I thought to myself. It wasn't until years later that I realized they were talking about people who weren't Jewish!

❖

At a young age, I loved to bowl. One day I saw a notice for a youth bowling league, which was to start soon. I couldn't wait to sign up. My friend, Bobby, was joining it along with a bunch of boys I knew from school. We had loads of fun for the three months it lasted. It was a good way to stay busy during the long northeastern winter.

The culmination of that joy was a banquet at the end of the season. I looked forward to attending that great event. Our team won the championship and was awarded trophies. By then, there was a special bond between all of us. It was a great feeling to be part of that group. I was elated with the dinner and the happy occasion. But suddenly, one of the guys who thought he was a comedian said, "Hey, have you seen the funny hats those stupid Jews wear? Look at me; I'm a Jew boy!" He continued to mock as he placed a folded napkin on his head.

Most of the group roared with laughter. I felt like I had taken a blow to the gut and had the wind totally knocked out of me. I was completely shocked. I had never heard anything like this before. I had no idea anyone was persecuted because of their religion. I was silent as the pain seared my young heart. I was the only Jew there, and I don't think anyone knew it except my friend, Bobby.

I privately asked him afterward, "Why were they making fun of Jews?"

"Don't worry about it, Morey!" he consoled. "They're just a bunch of dummies." But I was profoundly wounded.

I did poorly in school since I didn't pay attention and was always misbehaving. I think the real problem was that I was hyperactive. All my teachers had me sit in the front row so that they could keep their eyes on me. I had almost perfect attendance in the principal's office. I really excelled in sports, though. When I was nine, I started to play on American Legion baseball teams and received trophies for being the best hitter in the league twice. Later, I played on the baseball and basketball teams in high school and set a record for the longest hitting streak in baseball when I got a hit in every game for two straight years.

My childhood seemed to be all fun and games with no responsibility until that fateful day when I was nine, and my father gave me some very bad news, "Morris, you must enroll in Hebrew school." Up until that time, there had been almost no religious instruction in my life.

I remember seeing the headlines of a newspaper about the Cold War between Russia and the U.S. I was troubled, and my mother tried to comfort me. She told me not to worry because everything was fate, and your time to die was set by God. She also informed me that there was no afterlife, so we needed to make the most of this life. I felt like I was making the most of it—having all the fun I could!

I lived for those neighborhood ball games after school each day. Talk about getting my wings clipped! I hated school, and now instead of being free to play ball afterward, I was forced to go to more school at the Synagogue for two hours a session three days a week. It felt unbearable, especially to a hyper kid like I was. So naturally, the rabbi had his hands full with me!

The first rabbi to teach my class, Rabbi Greenstein, was already in his seventies. He was very nice, but we boys were rotten. With all our bad behavior, I think we literally drove him to an early grave. One day we arrived at class and heard that he had passed away! But we knew no remorse.

His replacements were our worst nightmare. It was a husband and wife team who came from another planet where they didn't believe in using deodorant. The wife looked like Larry of *The Three Stooges*. They had no control in the classroom and were yelling at us constantly. When they were irritated, they would move in close and the odor was unbearable!

I was the ringleader of the troublemakers and received the brunt of the torture. I pleaded with my parents to let me quit Hebrew School, but they forced me to continue. Fortunately, those teachers were eventually dismissed.

We couldn't wait to meet our next teacher. Our goal wasn't to complete the course but to drive him out as we'd done with others. Rabbi Kuperstein was a man in his forties about six feet tall and rather muscular. He came through the door with absolute authority, and we quickly found out we'd met our match. He told us his story, how he had escaped from a Nazi concentration camp through an underground tunnel. The games were over, and the serious training began. We'd hardly learned anything in the first two years there, so we now had a little over a year to learn the Hebrew language and the approximately forty songs we'd have to sing at our Bar Mitzvah.

Ours was a Reform synagogue. In the Orthodox tradition, students are required to learn the Torah, the first five books of the Hebrew Scriptures (which are also the first five books of the Christian Bible). Reform Jews are "only" required to perform the rituals of singing, about forty prayers and the Haftorah, a series of selections from the Hebrew prophets.

My big day came when I turned thirteen at the end of March. My rabbi was a cantor, and he had a beautiful voice. To say I didn't have a cantor's voice would be one of the greatest understatements of the century. There was no music in our home, and I couldn't even make the choir at my school. Somehow, though, I had deceived myself into thinking I was Elvis. Imagine being in front of about a hundred people and having to chant forty songs in a strange language with no musical accompaniment. I couldn't carry a tune to save my life, and to make matters worse, my voice was changing at that time. I sang my heart out, not realizing how terrible I sounded. The horrible squeaking and cracking of my voice sent my three older sisters into convulsions of laughter. And to add insult to injury, my classmates, who were supposed to join in with me, remained stone silent throughout the ordeal. Looking back, I recall my mother slipping me a valium before it all began to calm my nerves. I suppose that may have slowed me down a bit!

When I finally finished, the rabbi told the whole congregation, "He did very well despite his voice." I was crushed and vowed never to sing in public again. My mother was so angry at the rabbi, she told him off. Well, at least I'd become a man, and I did receive a lot of gifts on this celebrated day, which helped soothe my pain and humiliation. In fact, I received enough money to buy a new car, which I did when I turned seventeen.

CHAPTER FOUR

Teenage Years

When I turned sixteen and finally passed my driver's test after several failed attempts, my father bought me a car. This may not have been the wisest thing he ever did, but of course, I didn't comprehend that back then. What teenage boy wouldn't be thrilled to get his own set of wheels? The problem was that this set of wheels wasn't put together very well. It was a 1961 Rambler. He literally bought it from an old lady for $250.

People immediately started telling me stories of how they were at the bottom of a hill and saw wheels come rolling down at them—Rambler wheels that had come off! I ignored these stories hoping they weren't true. I had a more immediate concern. I didn't know how to drive a standard, and neither did anyone else in my family. I also didn't know anything about cars and couldn't ask my father because he didn't even know how to check the oil in his car. The first time I took the Rambler for a drive, smoke started coming out of the engine. I jumped out of the car and ran for my life, thinking it was going to explode. After a while, it stopped smoking, and I got back in and drove home. My friend put some oil in the car and solved the problem. Fortunately, (or maybe, unfortunately) for me, my good friend, Jeff, knew how to drive a standard. Jeff was another wild kid, a speedster who could have qualified for the Indy 500.

A bunch of us decided to skip school to go to our high school soccer tournament. I handed Jeff the car keys. This was a huge mistake. On the way back from the game, he decided to drag race with a girl from our school. She slowed down, and he passed her. Then he noticed the thruway exit, and going about 80 mph, he executed the turn, which only a highly skilled driver could have done. When we pulled up to the toll booth, we were notified that the state trooper wanted to speak to us about the crazy driving. Jeff had a different plan. He faked like he was going to pull over but then peeled out. We heard a siren screaming and saw lights flashing. Somehow, he managed to pull into an alley, and we lost him. He then handed me the keys and demanded that I drive home, which I refused to do since I still hadn't learned to drive a standard. He told me he had outrun police cars on five previous occasions. His father owned a car dealership, and every Saturday night, he would take a different car out for a joy ride! I rode with him one time when he was going over 100 mph!

After the thruway episode, I was paranoid that I was going to be arrested sooner or later. The phone rang one day, and a man said, "This is the police let me speak to your mother." I quickly confessed to my mother about the escapade. To my relief, it was only a neighbor playing a practical joke.

A bunch of guys and I ordered pizza another night and hopped into my Rambler to go pick it up when suddenly, the front wheel fell off. Imagine what would have happened to us if that had occurred during the drag racing.

Angels and an Orange Fiat

After my Rambler was declared totaled because of the axle breaking, I decided to spend the two thousand dollars I'd received from my Bar Mitzvah on a new car.

The year was 1968. My parents took me to a local car dealership, and the minute I saw the bright, orange, convertible Fiat Spider, I knew I'd found the car for me. Mom and Dad tried to steer me in a more conservative direction but to no avail. My mind was made up!

I felt I had gone from rags to riches. When I was ten, I was the only kid around without a bicycle. I begged my parents for a bike, but with six kids and a very modest income, times were tough. I had to wait until I was eleven, which seemed like an eternity. Now I was the only teenager in the school with a brand-new convertible.

My parents instructed me to drive safely and made me promise that I would never let anyone else drive it. Too bad I didn't listen!

It was a cold wintry night when my buddy, Ron, and I drove to a bar in Saratoga Springs. We had a few drinks and then decided to go home. We were a little too late! We walked out into a blizzard. Ron decided he should drive back, so I handed him the keys. The snow was so heavy we could barely see the road, and we were going way too fast. We weren't halfway home when Ron missed a curve in the road, and we went flying over a cliff. It felt like we were riding a snow machine going down a very steep hill. Good thing Ron didn't panic and just let the car fly over the embankment. We heard the scraping and banging of my new wheels as it hit many large rocks on the way down. We finally came to a stop at the bottom of a ravine.

I can't believe the car didn't flip! There must have been angels protecting us as there is no way a car could go down such a steep grade without overturning. The Bible says we all have guardian angels (Psalm 91:11). I think they must have been working overtime that night.

Thankfully, a man with a truck and a large chain pulled us out before the police came, or we would have been arrested for DWI. At the age of eighteen, we took chances we shouldn't have. Drinking and driving are always wrong, and going out in a blizzard is very dangerous.

I can only say that God had mercy on us! As we drove home, we heard all kinds of terrible noises coming from underneath the vehicle. My mother took it to the garage the next day, and they told her the car was totaled because the frame was bent. She called me at work screaming, "What did you do to that car? It's ruined!"

My heart was broken since I loved that little car. But Ron and I had miraculously escaped without any injuries, and we were grateful to be alive.

I guess I started drinking to compensate for my insecurity and to try to fit in since I was also an introvert. I was only sixteen, and I was drinking hard liquor. I would get drunk and become loud and boisterous. I thought I was cool, but I was really making a fool of myself. It got so bad that after a Friday night binge, I was still drunk when I arrived for my Saturday morning baseball game. I didn't even realize this until I parked my car and almost went over a cliff. I knew that if my coach found out about my drinking, I'd be thrown off the team! One time, another team's coach had seen me at a bar.

When I stepped up to the plate, he yelled, "Hey number three, are you going to the Beachcomber tonight?" I struck out on three pitches to stop his attack.

Sometimes friends who are willing to tell us the truth about ourselves can have a major impact on our lives. One night when I was at a bar with my buddy, Dale, he pointed to a despicable looking drunk and said, "Morey, unless you stop drinking, you're going to be just like him." His words pierced my heart like a dagger. I then quit drinking for two reasons: it made me sick, and I didn't want to end up like that disgusting bum.

❖

Graduating from high school presents all kinds of problems for a teenager with no purpose or direction for the future. I'd dreamed of playing major league baseball, but that bubble burst when some professional scouts watched my game and determined that I was too small and didn't have enough arm strength.

So, I enrolled in college with an accounting major because math had always been my best subject. For years I had gotten my whole identity from playing sports. I had been a star athlete at a small high school and basked in the glory of that acclaim and subsequent popularity.

Now that was all gone, and I had to start all over again at college. It was a difficult transition. It truly felt overwhelming to me. I became depressed and started smoking marijuana.

This was the tail end of the sixties, and the hippie movement was still in full swing. I had a beard and grew my blonde hair to my shoulders. I looked like General Custer. But to add to my gloom, I started losing my hair at the age of eighteen. Everyone loves to poke fun at bald people, but that can be really hurtful, especially when it happens at such a young age.

I tried to mask my insecurity by acting cool, but I still felt totally empty inside. These were some of the hardest times I'd experienced up to that point in my life. I got so depressed that I barely spoke at all to anyone. All I wanted to do was sleep, play basketball, and get high. Marijuana is a very deceptive drug and makes everything seem to go in slow motion. I've always loved watching football except when I was smoking pot since it slowed everything down and made me see how violent the sport really is!

In my rebellious state, I skipped a lot of classes and would have flunked out of college if I hadn't been the star basketball player. My teammates knew they couldn't win the championship without me, so they started a cheating ring to help pull me through. They wrote my papers for me and even went so far as to distract the professor in the middle of the exam so we could exchange papers. The teacher's office was close to the classroom, so we commissioned one guy to call her and then traded papers when she left the room.

I'm not proud of who I was then or what I did. I managed to graduate from college, though, and we won the championship in basketball. While these accomplishments were gratifying, I had no peace in my heart and still felt very empty.

It was around this time that I went to a drug party and met a girl who was as messed up as I was. I had never had a girlfriend or dated much. I didn't have a lot of confidence in that area. The only things we had in common were drugs and the hippie scene. I was too into getting high to have any discernment, and I was leading an immoral lifestyle. She claimed to be pregnant, so I felt I had to marry her. This was a false claim. So, with me at the ripe old age of twenty and her at only eighteen, we found ourselves shackled together in a union that neither one of us wanted. We had no attraction or love for one another. All we had was hatred and resentment, so the marriage was a living hell.

CHAPTER FIVE

Basic Training

I thought things couldn't get any worse until I received a draft notice and was in danger of being sent to Vietnam. I enlisted in the Air Force and was sent to San Antonio, Texas, where they immediately cut off all my long hair. (Most of which never grew back!)

Basic training can be rough for anybody, but for me, it was a total nightmare. When they took us to the rifle range to teach us the basics about the M-16 rifle, I wasn't too thrilled. I once sank thirty-seven free throws in a row at the gym, but I knew I was no sharpshooter. In fact, my father never owned any guns, and I had no experience with them. The target was large and about fifty feet away.

The sergeant said, "Anyone who can't hit the target is an idiot." We had sixty shots and needed fifty hits to pass the test. Everything went wrong for me! First, my glasses fogged up so badly, I could hardly see the target. And the rifle had a little kick to it, which I felt in my shoulder, causing me to jerk quite a bit.

After we were done shooting, we checked our targets, and almost everyone had fifty or sixty hits. One guy even set a record with sixty-six. This was because he was next to me! My target had only sixteen hits, which was the lowest ever recorded. They made me go to remedial training, where everybody tried to get next to me so that I'd hit their targets. I doubled my score and hit thirty-three winners.

But after the sergeant yelled, "Time's up!" I pulled the trigger one last time, which was a huge mistake. The sergeant went ballistic, screaming in my ear and told me to leave the site immediately and never come back.

This was just the beginning of my troubles. I had been brought up with no responsibilities or work ethic. My only requirement at home was to hang up my coat, and I didn't usually even do that. I had a drill sergeant who was five feet eight and 220 pounds of solid muscle. He also had an extremely loud voice and was screaming at me constantly. I had no trouble with the physical workouts, but keeping everything in order was totally foreign to me.

Every morning at four a.m., they would switch the lights on and shout at us to get moving and be ready for inspection in thirty minutes. The bed had to be perfectly made so you could bounce a dime off of it. I'd never made a bed in my life! We had to be in uniform with our shoes shined. Our lockers and drawers had to be minutely organized and were inspected. The first couple of weeks, I failed every inspection. And, unfortunately for them, the whole troop was repeatedly punished if one guy failed. Everybody hated me because they had to suffer for my total incompetence.

We never knew what to expect from day to day in basic training. Sunday was approaching, and we were hoping for a day to relax. There is no such thing in basic training!

After we arose at four a.m. and had breakfast, the sergeant asked, "Does anyone want to attend religious services?" Only two airmen raised their hands.

The sergeant released them, then sadistically smiled at the rest of us and said, "You're all going on K.P. duty." This was not what we wanted to do on Sunday. It was tedious work; washing dishes, taking out the trash, and mopping floors while somebody railed on you the whole time for being too slow.

So naturally, the next Sunday, when our leader asked, "Does anyone want to go to church?" We all raised our hands. We eagerly marched over to the house of worship. I didn't know what to expect, never having attended a church service in my life. I was curious to check this out.

The Chaplin was very organized and told us to get in two lines, one for Catholics and the other for Protestants. When he saw me standing by myself, looking confused, he probably thought that I was a troublemaker.

"What's your problem, airman? Isn't either line good enough for you?"

I responded, "Sir, I'm Jewish."

"Hmm, we've never had this problem before," he mused with a furrowed brow. "Go in my office and pick out a book to read," he ordered.

I miraculously graduated from basic training with a lot of help from my friends. Then the Lord had mercy on me. Due to my total lack of military skills, and since I had a degree in accounting, I was given a cushy job in the finance office. Therefore, while others were flying planes in combat, I stayed stateside.

After about a year, however, I received notice that I was headed to Southeast Asia in ninety days. A huge chill went down my spine when I received the news. But again, God had mercy on me. Just before I was scheduled to leave, President Nixon ended the war. I was able to stay in Mississippi to complete my four years of service.

While finishing my duty there, I joined a bunch of guys for some touch football after work. I received the kickoff and had one man to beat for the touchdown. I faked left, and my right knee gave out. It was the worst pain I'd ever felt in my life. I couldn't even walk.

The military hospital didn't have any orthopedics there, so they decided to put a cast on me. The only problem was that the person who did it had never wrapped a cast in his life. He just kept wrapping and wrapping. It must have weighed fifty pounds by the time he finished. I could barely lift my leg off the ground. When the doctor saw it the next day, he burst out laughing and had it rewrapped. Funny for him.

The cast was finally removed six weeks later, but after my knee slipped out half a dozen times, and they put a new cast on me after every incident, they finally decided I should see an orthopedic surgeon. The closest one to Columbus, Mississippi, was in Montgomery, Alabama, about three hours away. I had to take a bus and bring my medical records in a large manila folder. I was quite concerned when they dropped me off at a bus station instead of at the hospital. I didn't know what to do. Then I spotted a number of young men carrying manila folders just like mine. *What a lucky break*, I thought, and followed them onto a bus. We rode quite a while, and then we approached their destination. When I saw the sign, I was really alarmed. This wasn't a hospital but an Army base! They were all new recruits who were just arriving on base. How was I going to get out of this mess? It was basic training all over again!

"Sit down and shut up!" the sergeant bellowed. I patiently waited to tell him—you've got the wrong man here. I raised my hand, but he barked, "No questions! Just shut up and listen. You're in the Army now! We ship out tomorrow morning after breakfast, so you better be prepared." What a nightmare! After graduating from basic training, the last thing you want to do is go back again. Finally, I couldn't take it any longer, and I stood up.

He yelled, "Sit down!"

I refused to obey, so they escorted me out of the room, thinking I was a rebel. I finally got them to listen, and they just shook their heads. They made me stay the night, fed me grits for breakfast as my punishment, and then drove me to the hospital. They commanded me never to enter an army base like that again, to which I gave them my solemn promise.

I thought my nightmare was over until I arrived at the hospital. Military hospitals in the 1970s were as crazy as the *M*A*S*H* TV series.

The surgeon was a Jew and asked me, "What is a nice Jewish boy doing in the military?"

When I told him I was in the finance department, he laughed, knowing Jewish people really like money.

There wasn't any arthroscopic surgery in those days, so he had to cut into the knee surgically to repair the torn meniscus.

After the surgery, I was in the worst pain of my life. The pain pills and shots only lasted two hours, and they could only give them to me every four hours. I can remember staying up all night because of the intense pain and watching the sunrise in the morning. I finally dozed off but was abruptly awakened to eat breakfast after only one hour of sleep.

I was in a room with eight other guys who'd all had surgery. Only one guy could get out of bed, so he controlled what we watched on TV. He loved watching big-time wrestling and would torture us with it for hours. We begged and pleaded with him to change the station, but he just smiled and kept his eyes glued to the set.

I met an African American man who had been in the service nineteen years and could have retired after one more year of service, but they sent him to Selma, Alabama, and he went AWOL. There were a lot of race riots in that area then, and he didn't feel safe there.

I couldn't lift my leg even one inch when they took me to therapy. The young recruits working there were not qualified to be therapists. They were sadistic as they held my leg up in the air and told me, "We're going to let go if you don't hold it up." I was in tremendous pain and too weak to hold my leg up. I pleaded with them for mercy, but they just laughed. Obviously, they loved to torment their patients. I had to endure two weeks of this agony before I was released from that madhouse.

CHAPTER SIX

A New Life

I was twenty-two, and my life felt horribly empty. I tried to fill the void with some temporary pleasures like drugs and parties, but these things didn't satisfy the ache in my heart.

I can remember when I went to see the movie *The Ten Commandments*. I was so deeply touched by the film that I thought I would become a rabbi. This desire lasted about thirty minutes and my short dream disappeared, but I think a seed of faith was planted in my heart. At the time, I didn't realize the significance of my name: Morris and Moses are synonymous.

I met some college students from a group called Campus Crusade for Christ, who tried to share their faith with me. All they said was "Jesus loves you" and asked me to read a pamphlet called the Four Spiritual Laws. It didn't make any sense to me. I still didn't understand much about Jesus or why I needed to.

I was driving north to visit my family in upstate New York during my winter break. When I reached Syracuse, there was a terrible snowstorm. There were many cars off the road, and I feared for my life.

I really prayed from my heart for the first time in my life, "God, if you save me from this blizzard, I'll believe in you." If you pray to God with an honest heart, He will hear you and answer you. Psalm 50:15 says (NKJV), "Call upon me in the day of trouble; I will deliver you, and you shall glorify Me."

I arrived safely at a motel. I opened a drawer and saw a Bible. I opened it to the book of Matthew and became really upset because all I saw were genealogies. I slammed it shut and thought, who wants to follow a God like this.

When I arrived back at the base, I started physical therapy. My therapist, Mike Parker, was a super friendly guy. Somehow, we got on the subject of religion. I told him I was Jewish, thinking that would be the end of the discussion. This had always been my experience in the past. No one back home in New York had ever talked to me about their Christian faith. I had recently overheard another airman telling his friend about Jesus and what a difference his faith had made in his life. But when I approached this guy and told him I wanted to hear about Jesus, he was resistant.

"What religion are you?" he queried.

"I'm Jewish," I replied.

"Sorry, but I'm not allowed to share this with you," he insisted.

So, when Mike's eyes lit up, and he openly shared his faith in Christ, I was shocked. At first, I was a little hesitant to believe the gospel message, but he gave me a few books to read, which made a huge difference. One was the New Testament of the Christian Bible. When I read the Gospel of John, my heart nearly exploded with excitement. I had been an agnostic, but now my eyes were opened to the truth of Christ's love and sacrifice.

I accepted Jesus as the Jewish Messiah and opened my heart to Him. It was like a lightning bolt. In an instant of time, I received hope and salvation. I had a new purpose in life and no longer feared death because of Christ's resurrection. It was wonderful to know that this life is not the end, as I had been raised to believe. Now I knew there was a heaven, and better yet, I could know for certain that I was headed there because Christ paid for my sins when He became the sacrificial Passover lamb and died on the cross.

I wanted to share my newfound faith and joy with everyone I met, but only a few responded. I shared the good news of Christ with an African American man named Gene. He was very receptive and started reading the Bible that I gave him. He loved the book of Exodus, especially the freeing of the Jewish slaves. I wanted to invite him to visit a church with me, but when I talked to a man at work about this, he told me that blacks were not welcome at "white churches" in that area. I was appalled to see that racism was still so rampant in the South, even in the '70s.

I hadn't yet learned much about hearing God's voice or being led by the Holy Spirit, but I know God spoke to my heart to make a trip back home to New York to visit my family and to share the Gospel with my brother Jeffrey.

The situation didn't look too promising when I first arrived there. I found Jeff at a party with his friends drinking and smoking dope. When I tried to share the Gospel with them, they openly ridiculed me. One guy held up his beer bottle and loudly proclaimed, "This is my god!" A teenage girl said, "If you knew what happened to me, you wouldn't believe in God." I told them that God loved them without responding to their cynicism.

The next day my brother approached me privately and exclaimed, "They're all fools! I want what you have!" So I gave him a Gospel of John booklet to read, and when he reached the fifth chapter, his eyes lit up just as mine had, and he asked Jesus to come into his heart and forgive his sins.

Jeff and I had always had a good relationship, but now we had a real spiritual bond, which made us even closer. He came to see me in Mississippi on his college break, and he was deeply burdened about our father. He also thought that Jesus would be returning before the month was over. (New converts can get carried away with zeal!)

Neither one of us had told our parents about our conversion yet, and it weighed on us heavily. Following the tradition of Jacob, the biblical schemer, we came up with a plan. Did we pray and ask for God's wisdom and direction? No. We were still too confident in the flesh for that. Also, Jeff had a real fear that was driving him. He had seen my father almost choke to death recently, and he was afraid he would die soon without coming to know Christ. Therefore, we decided to take the easy way out and wrote him a letter explaining that Jesus is the Jewish Messiah.

There are over three hundred prophecies in the Jewish scriptures that portray Christ as the Messiah, so it took nine pages for us to cover all the evidence. We decided to mail this letter to my father's workplace since we were concerned my mother would otherwise intercept it and keep it from him. Well, we all know what happens to the best-laid plans of mice and men. For some reason, my father's boss, who was also a Jew, opened the letter and read it before Dad got a hold of it. He then very tactfully informed my father, "It sounds like your son is involved in some kind of religious cult."

My poor father was totally humiliated, along with being shocked and horrified at the news about his sons! He rejected our beliefs and severely admonished us to never broach that subject with him again. We respected his wishes but continued to pray for him. I did challenge him at one point, "Would you have been happier if we had stayed on drugs?" He didn't reply.

Years later, when I thought my father had left the room, I shared the Gospel with my mother and sister for about an hour. Afterward, I asked my mother, "Where did Dad go?"

"He's sitting right behind you!" she laughingly retorted. He had listened politely without saying a word.

While in Mississippi, I was asked to speak at churches, and everyone loved hearing about my Jewish background and subsequent conversion. When I was twenty-three, I felt God calling me into the ministry. Fortunately, my Air Force commitment was now complete. I looked into a number of Bible schools, but they all seemed to have too many rules that smacked of legalism, such as no dancing, playing cards, or watching movies. So, I enrolled in Mississippi State University with a major in ministerial studies. It was a busy and exciting time of growth. I was working forty hours a week and going to college full-time, yet I was able to make the dean's list because I loved to study now.

When God places a calling on our lives, there are always tests and trials along the way. Sadly, most people never learn to hear God's voice well. Parents should train their children in this area at a young age. I obviously hadn't received that training. Although I was very zealous, I had a lot to learn about following God. Jesus was led into the wilderness by the Holy Spirit to be prepared for ministry. He passed the test in forty days. "And you shall remember that the Lord your God led you all the way these forty years in the wilderness, to humble you and test you, to know what was in your heart..." (Deuteronomy 8:2 NKJV). Never did I imagine it would take twenty-five years for me to fulfill my calling of becoming a pastor. But bad decisions can lead to delays in your life's mission, and I made a lot of them.

I only had one year left to finish my degree at the university, when I became very disillusioned with my studies. I had learned that most of the theology department there espoused the doctrine of Calvinism. My Western Civilization professor was a gifted teacher and came to class one day impersonating John Calvin. This made an enormous impression on me. Calvin believed in the doctrine of predestination, which teaches that

God elects only a limited number of souls to be saved. In other words, he believed that God doesn't give everyone the ability to respond to His plan of salvation. That didn't sound like the Jesus of the Bible to me then, and it still doesn't today. We know that according to the Scriptures, Jesus is full of love, compassion, mercy, and grace. 2 Peter 3:9 (KJV) teaches that God is "...not willing that any should perish, but that all should come to repentance."

Jesus also taught us the way to discern false teachers. In Matthew, Chapter 7:16 (NKJV), He said, "You will know them by their fruits." I looked at the fruit of John Calvin's life by reading his biography. Calvin established a theocracy in Geneva, Switzerland, where the church ruled the state, and they had thirty-four people burned at the stake for doctrinal differences, which they called heresy ("Calvin's Reign of Terror" 2020). When one man cried out, "Jesus, save me!" Calvin replied, "If he had addressed Him as Lord Jesus, I would have extinguished the flames" (Bala 2017). Calvin thought if he could rid the world of one heretic, he could keep a hundred people from being deceived. Obviously, this was not Christian love!

My disillusionment with Calvinism was a strong factor in my decision to leave the college but not the only one. My brother Jeff had embarked on his own spiritual journey. He dropped out of college and enrolled in a small Bible school located just thirty miles from our hometown. I had visited the church connected to this Bible school when I had been home and loved it. This was the era of the Jesus People Movement: a wave of spiritual awakening, which collided with the hippie movement all across the nation. Since I still had quite a bit of hippie in me, I was drawn to it like a magnet, as were millions of young people back then. It was a true move of God's Spirit to bring salvation to a generation that had veered way off course. There were throngs of young people attending the church and school my brother went to, and everyone was full of excitement. There was also a greater freedom of the Spirit there than at any other church I had visited previously. There was nothing of the stiff high church formality and ritualism that was and still is prevalent in most Christian houses of worship. The Biblical church pattern is for much participation by the congregation in every service (1 Corinthians14:26). This was evident there as well as people moving in the gifts of the Holy Spirit, such as prophecy and healing.

Jeff had been trying to get me to follow his example and enroll in the Bible school. I definitely wasn't crazy about Mississippi and wanted to be closer to family. So, I left MSU to become a Bible school student in upstate

New York. I couldn't wait to start classes. It was a night school, which worked well for me since I now had a family to support.

CHAPTER SEVEN

A Tough Transition

As soon as I moved back to New York, everything went wrong. I couldn't find a job anywhere. I was looking for work in my field of accounting when I applied for a position with a toy manufacturer. They had nothing in finance, but they said they were hiring in the factory. This was the last thing I wanted, especially since it was the second shift and would keep me from starting Bible school. But, feeling desperate, I filled out an application and then waited for an interview. There was a long line of applicants. A few moments later, the supervisor appeared. He had seen my application with my degree and experience in accounting. He said, "Hire him! Accountants are brilliant!"

What he didn't realize was that though I excelled with numbers, I had absolutely no mechanical ability, which was exactly what the job required. He soon found out he had made a big mistake when it took me three full hours to assemble a pinball machine. As he watched me closely and noticed the trouble I had just hammering nails, he asked, "Have you used a hammer much in your life?"

"Very rarely," I truthfully confessed, my face turning beet red. They tried to pressure me to work faster, which made me think that for minimum wage, *who needs this hassle.*

I soon quit that job when my brother-in-law got me hired at the milk dairy where he worked. And, no, this wasn't in finance either! Though it paid fairly well, this job was excruciating in every respect. Once again, my total lack of mechanical skills made me the worst possible candidate they could have found for the position. And it was also second shift, so again I had to put off starting Bible school.

My first job there was moving crates of milk, which weighed fifty pounds apiece. These crates were wet, so naturally, I was too, which made me especially miserable since I was in a cooler where the temperature was forty degrees. You can imagine my relief when my eight-hour shift finally ended. But they told me, "You're here till we finish!" I can remember working seventeen hours one day. At one point, I had to work all twelve-hour shifts for thirty-three straight days. And someone

asked me why I looked tired! It felt like I was an Israel-
ite under Pharaoh's reign!

After a year of this torture, I was "promoted" to
running milk machines and even managed to secure
a third shift position. Yippie! This was good because I
had decided I was going to start Bible school, whether
they fired me or not. The maintenance men, who were
overworked, would scream at me every time I called for
help, which was several times each night. They'd shout,
"I'm too busy! Why don't you fix it?" It was extremely
humiliating! It was also mind-numbingly tedious since
I had to stay by myself for twelve hours just watching a
machine.

I asked God, "What are you trying to teach me?" I
don't remember getting an answer then. Now I understand that He wanted to make me humble and help me
learn to be with Him and pray.

Hasidic Rabbi

One day at the plant, I was approached by a Hasidic
Rabbi, whose job was to make sure we processed the
milk according to Kosher procedures. He was dressed
in the traditional black and white garb and had a long
beard. He was from Brooklyn, where they say there are
more Jews than in Israel.

When he learned from my sister that I was a Messianic Jew, he was outraged.

"Your father and your whole family are going to hell!" he raved. I was astounded at the anger in his voice and what he was saying. I was always ready for a good debate. I was young and arrogant and full of head knowledge. I challenged him right away with a question.

"By the way, where do you offer your sacrifices now?" quoting a reference from Psalm 40:6. He threw his hands up in the air, "We have no temple!" he said very emotionally. He followed me around for three hours as we exchanged jabs.

I quoted Isaiah 53 to him, which describes the crucifixion of the Messiah seven hundred fifty years before the birth of Christ. Most synagogues will not allow this passage to be read during their services. His mind was set; he was not open to believing that Jesus was the Messiah. I asked him, "Do you love truth or tradition?"

"Your father is going to hell because of your conversion!" he ranted. I was making progress because now the whole family wasn't going to hell.

After three hours of dialogue, I decided to pose this question to him, "Would you pray and ask God to show you the truth?" He responded with a silly joke about Christians and told me his faith was in Moses.

I asked him, "How many thousands of years ago did Moses live? There is more historical evidence about Jesus, who was born two thousand years ago than Moses, who lived four thousand years ago." He finally relented in his argument and said,

"All religions are based on faith." He then walked away and never criticized me again.

CHAPTER EIGHT

Deception

I was very excited to be in Bible School at last. Everything seemed wonderful there for the first year. There was tremendous teaching, worship, and fellowship. The pastor, a single man in his mid-thirties, was very creative and allowed a lot of freedom in the church. Anyone could share a song, teaching, or prophecy. Things seemed to be going according to the scriptural pattern with much participation from the congregation (1 Corinthians 14:26), and I was extremely happy with it.

As time went on, though, I began noticing some discrepancies with the pastor and one of the other teachers. The pastor was leading the church to believe that we were the special group that was on a much higher level than any other church. He claimed we had deeper revelations and understanding of Scripture than other groups.

Then I began seeing signs that made me wonder if I had joined a cult. The Pastor, Derek, chose twelve elders and gave them special communion cups. He also claimed to be the father of a new movement and seemed to desire to be called father. The more I examined things in the light of the Scripture, the more red flags I saw.

Pastor Derek, who had grown up in a Pilgrim Holiness Church, absolutely abhorred all tradition and detested all the mainline Christian denominations. One night, as I listened to him preaching, he became extremely angry, and his tone turned nasty.

"All denominations are sinful!" he shouted.

One man then stood up and opposed him, "Why can't we all be in unity?" he questioned sincerely.

This only seemed to fan the flame of the pastor's wrath. "Get out of here and don't ever come back!" he yelled at the man. He later explained to me privately that this man was a Baptist, and he had purposefully singled him out in his message to get rid of him! I was horrified.

I attempted to talk to the elders and other church members about the problems I had observed, but no one would listen. It was like they were under a spell. Another unscriptural issue with the church was that none of the elders were, in fact, elder. Most were in their early twenties, and a couple were in their thirties. They obviously had no real maturity or experience. They could be easily deceived. It was similar in that sense to the

Mormon church, where they send out young people in their twenties to evangelize and give them the title elder. Actually, there were very few older people in the entire church. It was almost all young people in their teens or twenties, a totally opposite situation from most churches today.

I continued to observe that anyone who challenged the pastor was thrown out of the church and that anyone who left was humiliated from the pulpit.

I had just completed the two-year course there and was about to be ordained and become a teacher when a terrible scandal caused the church and school to explode almost as if a bomb had been dropped on it. It was revealed that the pastor was a homosexual and had been accused of molesting students as well as teenage boys from the congregation. And if that wasn't horrible enough, it was also discovered that the pastor and some of the other members had become drug users. I personally heard the story from the young student who had instigated this destructive behavior. He admitted giving the pastor a then popular book on employing drug use to attain "deeper revelations" from God. Once Derek began experimenting with drugs, he underwent a complete personality change and became a raving lunatic. He also linked his drug use to Transcendental Meditation, which is occultic in nature.

The breakup of the church and school, which swiftly followed, was devastating to me and to scores of others. Many lost their faith and never recovered. My brother left town without telling me and abandoned the ministry. I stopped attending church because my heart was broken. I gave up my dream of being a pastor and left my first love, Jesus. I didn't return to church for eight years. I had put my faith in a church and a movement instead of in the Lord.

At that time, I was young and naive like the other Bible school students, so though I saw many warning signs, I didn't comprehend the big picture as clearly as I do today. I have since done some research on the subject of cults, and it's incredible how many typical cult characteristics were manifested through Derek and the church.

Cults are generally led by someone with a charismatic personality, which Derek had. Leaders are often motivated by the lust for sex and power. This was obviously proven to be true in his case. Cult leaders want to control their member's personal decisions and limit their ability to make choices for themselves. They tend to manipulate people through guilt, shame, and fear. This was also evident with Derek.

The church had established a number of communes where members could live. It was not mandatory, but this environment was promoted and appealed to the young, single, Bible school students in particular. I can see where this set up gave the pastor more opportunity to exercise control over them.

One major area where Derek asserted his authority to dominate people was in the planning of marriages. He demanded that prospective couples get his approval before forming a union. A close friend of mine went to him for counseling regarding this matter, wanting to wed a certain woman. Derek refused to approve his choice and afterward arranged for another man to marry this woman. This marriage dissolved within a year, leaving the young woman traumatized and so disillusioned that she left the faith. I saw many more of these arranged marriages quickly fall apart as well. "Unless the Lord builds the house, those who build it labor in vain" (Psalm 127:1 ESV).

Derek was what the Bible calls a wolf in sheep's clothing (Matthew 7:15). He abused his position and power, and tragically many lives were destroyed as a result. I had personally observed many souls shattered by the cult, but probably the saddest scenario was in the life of the cofounder, Jerry.

I met up with Jerry's daughter, Rose, at a Christian concert many years after the breakup of the group. She was excited about serving God and urged me to visit her father, making me aware of his needs. When I entered his home, though, I wasn't prepared for the pathetic sight of this once vibrant man. Jerry was now in his sixties and just a shell of his former self. He'd never been a large man, but it seemed he'd withered away to almost nothing now. Cancer had almost completely consumed him. He was so small and frail that I found it painful to look at him.

"Thanks for coming, Morey," he managed weakly.

"It's good to see you," I responded.

I sat down in a chair close to him, as I'd been told he'd become hard of hearing. We made a bit of small talk for a while, but I've found that most people eventually want to share their hearts. God calls us to bear one another's burdens, and one of the best ways to do this is to learn to be a good listener. This is a critically needed skill that few people have developed. My wife especially gets irritated with the way so many people habitually interrupt and try to finish other's sentences these days. Since I already knew a lot about his background and the church-turned-cult, I was truly interested in getting his perspective on that unfortunate chapter.

"I poured seven years of my life into that place, Morey. I was willing to give all for those folks. I genuinely cared about everyone there," he sighed heavily. His heart was still raw after forty years.

"Why did you leave?" I probed gently. I wanted to hear it from him personally, even though I already had my theories. And I think he needed to tell it.

"I knew Derek had some serious issues," he began. "I was trying to overlook as much as I could, praying that God would convict him and bring him around. One night, though, he finally went too far. He had called me to a meeting with him and some of the other elders. When I got there, I could tell they'd been smoking weed. One of the elders even handed me a joint. I threw it down, and then Derek got defensive. He told me it was okay; that God had given them a new revelation. He claimed that drugs would help us go deeper in the Spirit and that we would gain a higher level of enlightenment. I just couldn't believe it, Morey! I had to take a stand!" I could hear the panic in his voice.

"I told him that it was wrong, pure and simple. Then Derek flew into a rage and started railing on me. All those years, I thought we had a close relationship. It was over in a minute. But that wasn't the end. A few days later, during a church service, he badmouthed me to the entire congregation and ordered them to shun me, which they all did. People I had spent years ministering to wouldn't even speak to me. Even the kids wouldn't talk to me," He almost choked up remembering this. "They turned their heads away when I said hi."

"I'm really sorry, Jerry," I attempted to console him.

The pain was obviously intense, and my heart ached for him. But even sadder was the fact that he told me he was an agnostic now. He had turned away from the only One who could heal him from his bitter past. I pray for Jerry—that he would turn back to the Lord and receive "...the peace of God that passeth all understanding..." (Philippians 4:7 KJV). Additionally, I pray that he would cast his cares to the One who could identify with his pain. Jesus was "...despised and rejected of men; a man of sorrows and acquainted with grief..." (Isaiah 53:3 KJV).

CHAPTER NINE

Fall from Grace

My thirties were the worst years of my life. I had lost my faith, my job was miserable, and my marriage was horrific. It was an extremely depressing decade. I once again had no vision for the future. My only joy was in my three children, whom I loved dearly. I was working long hours at my job and had to grocery shop, cook, and care for them as well. It was incredibly rough, but God got us through, somehow. I wanted to be very involved in their lives since I hadn't received much attention from my parents. I coached my son's ball teams and got them all into playing lots of sports. They were very athletic, as I'd always been, so I really enjoyed watching them perform. I'm glad I could be there for my kids. It was a huge let down to me that my father hardly made it to any of my ball games and never took much of an interest in me.

These terribly difficult years were my Christian wilderness experience described in Deuteronomy 8:2—

God humbles us and tests us to see what's truly in our hearts. The purpose is for us to learn to rely on Him.

> *Trust in the Lord with all of your heart, and lean not unto your own understanding; In all your ways acknowledge Him, and He shall direct your paths.*
>
> (Proverbs 3:5–6 NKJV)

I didn't realize God was letting me hit rock bottom by reducing my confidence in my own ability. I was struggling financially to support three kids, and then the milk dairy suddenly closed down. I searched for a job for seven months without success. I finally took an exam for the post office and aced it. I had the top score for the Albany, NY District. I was hired by the Gloversville Post Office to be a letter carrier.

For the first seventy-five days of this job, you're on probation and have to meet their strict qualifications. Nobody knows how tough this job is unless they've tried it! It was January with frigid temperatures, and I had to walk about twelve miles a day carrying a forty-pound bag of mail. I did okay, though, and after about a month, everything was going smoothly until I got hurt playing basketball. I had a serious knee injury and needed surgery— again!

I should have been crying out to the Lord for comfort and strength, but I was still too full of pride. The first time the Lord got my attention was with a knee injury. Now He was allowing this to happen again, and I still didn't see it. I was called into the supervisor's office and fired because I couldn't perform the job. Three weeks later, the Schenectady Post Office hired me as a clerk, which was a blessing in disguise.

Shortly after this, my wife left me for another man, and we finally divorced, which in my case, was actually an enormous blessing, except for all the trauma my kids had to go through and the humiliation I endured. People have asked me... If your marriage was so awful, why didn't you divorce earlier? The simple answer is that I cared more about my children than my personal happiness. I'd seen how badly divorce affects kids. My best friend's parents divorced when we were young, and he was very depressed all the time. When my oldest sister's marriage broke up, my nephew was heartbroken. I had wanted to spare my kids that kind of pain.

The Bible states that there must be very serious grounds for divorce and, of course, there were in my case. I had every right to file for a divorce. Though two of my children were teenagers and the youngest was twelve, I knew it was still traumatic for them. Unfortunately, church people can be terribly judgmental on this subject, and incredibly, I experienced quite a bit of persecution from some Christians.

I was now officially a single dad. This was when God prepared me to be a pastor. Life's hardships make us see how much we need God. I already mentioned that I had quit attending church since the breakup of the Bible school. I thought I could be a Christian on my own, but I was failing miserably. After all I had been through, I finally got down on my knees and repented and cried out to God. All the peace I had lost for eight years came flooding back. God poured His grace out on me because my heart was finally right again. I now decided to look for another church. I knew I needed to get back in fellowship with other believers again, but I had no idea where to go.

CHAPTER TEN

New Beginnings

One day while channel surfing, I happened to flip on a local TV station, which was filming a revival service, and lo and behold, who was leading worship there but my old friend Greg Smith! Now I had my answer and knew where to attend church.

When I was twelve years old, we moved to a new neighborhood, and Greg was the first friend I made there. Sometimes God draws opposites together in friendship, perhaps to teach us by example. He and I were as different as night and day. His days were filled with responsibility and rigor, while mine were filled with freedom and frivolity. I was wild and reckless, and he was a boy scout. His time was almost completely structured with chores and piano lessons after school leaving little time for play. But thankfully, his parents allowed him to associate with the likes of me, and we did have fun in the spare time he had.

His was to be a lifelong friendship, which is a rare and precious commodity in our transient society. We stayed close until college and then lost touch with each other for about fifteen years. Now we were reunited in a special way when I showed up at his church one Sunday morning. Boy, was he shocked to see me walk through the door.

Tough Trials

Though I knew divorce was traumatic for kids, I wasn't prepared for the severe effect it had on my son, Jason. Jason had had various issues from a young age. He was borderline autistic and had a lot of trouble communicating. He could become violent when he was frustrated.

He did pretty well in school, though, and was a star athlete in football, basketball, and baseball. He scored twenty-six points in one high school basketball game. He could run like a deer and was timed at 4.6 seconds in the forty-yard dash in football, where he scored many touchdowns. Baseball was his best sport, and in batting practice, he hit seven balls over the fence, which was three hundred thirty feet from home plate. He was a natural athlete, and playing sports was his whole world.

After the divorce, though, he quit playing any sports and just wanted to stay in his room all the time. He became extremely depressed, and he completely shut down. I tried everything to motivate him to but to no avail. I was hoping and praying he would snap out of it, but he never did. Trauma, when not dealt with, can lead to mental illness.

No parent wants to see their child suffer like this. It's been a heavy burden for me to bear. He was diagnosed with schizophrenia and treated with chemicals instead of therapy. Sadly, the drugs he's been given for years have done nothing to improve his condition, and I still am praying for a miracle of healing in his life.

Being a single parent raising three teenagers is hard enough, but soon many problems arose, which seemed insurmountable. One day my youngest child, Joshua, came home and told me to take him to the doctor because he felt a lump in his stomach. The doctor thought it was only a water cyst. He said just to be safe, he would do exploratory surgery in six weeks. After the surgery, the doctor couldn't look me in the eye because he was afraid to tell me it was cancer. The word cancer can make anyone panic, but when it's your fifteen-year-old son, you want to scream at God and ask Him how He could allow this to happen.

They treated him with chemotherapy. It was the strongest dosage they could give him without killing him. He went through tremendous suffering, being sick all the time, along with losing his hair and fifty pounds.

I thought he was totally better after all the treatments until the doctor gave me more bad news.

"He has some spots on his lungs, and if there are five or more, we need to operate. There is still a tumor in his stomach. He may need twenty hours of surgery," he reported grimly. I was devastated, and to make matters worse, a friend called and gave me another negative report two days before the surgery.

"Morey, my husband had the same diagnosis as your son. They took out part of my husband's lung, and he had to learn how to breathe again!"

I tend to hold things in and have many defense mechanisms, but this was too much. I was angry with God. "Don't touch my son!" I cried out. It's funny how you lose all reason when someone is dear to your heart and suffering. I still went to church that night, and it was the best decision I ever made. The minute I walked into the sanctuary, I could feel God's presence. My wrath and anxiety melted into tears. I humbled myself and prayed a simple, selfish prayer, "Comfort me, Lord, I can't take it anymore!" Immediately I had a vision of Christ coming down from heaven and embracing me, and then I saw Him going to my son. After that experience, I had perfect peace. This is what the Bible calls the peace that passes all understanding (Philippians 4:7). I knew that with God's help, I could overcome anything.

"I can do all things through Christ which strengthens me" (Philippians 4:13 KJV). One of my favorite verses 2 Corinthians 1:3–4 (NIV) says, God is "...the God of all comfort, who comforts us in all our troubles, so that we can comfort those in any trouble..."

I traveled to New York City to the hospital, where the surgery was taking place. When I walked into my son's room, I was expecting the worst. I asked the nurse, "How did the lung surgery go?"

She replied, "There wasn't any!" I couldn't believe my ears! My heart was rejoicing. Jesus had not only comforted me, but He had healed Joshua's lungs. He did have surgery on his stomach, but that tumor was non-malignant. This all happened over twenty-five years ago, and he's in very good health today.

❖

Now that my relationship with the Lord was restored, everything began to fall into place. "The steps of a good man are ordered by the Lord..." (Psalm 37:23 KJV). I was still working third shift at the Schenectady Post Office, thirty miles from home. This was not a good situation for a single parent with three children. I felt trapped, but one day I saw a job opening at the Gloversville Post

Office. I was able to transfer there, and it was just a few minutes from my house.

My daughter, Jessica, was a real encouragement to me. She went to church with me, where I taught the teen Sunday School class, and she invited many of her friends to attend as well. One Sunday, I taught them that they were justified by faith alone (Ephesians 2:8–9). I explained to them that you can't earn your way to heaven. Christ's sacrifice on the cross was sufficient for us. I told them how certain denominations believed sacraments were necessary for salvation.

I didn't realize how stirred up these girls were until the next day when I picked them up from school. My daughter always volunteered me to drive her friends home. One girl who got in the car was Catholic. Another girl, who had attended my class, was riding with us and said to her, "Mr. Shapiro told us that some denominations think sacraments are required for a person to enter heaven." This young girl got quite angry and started yelling at her defensively. I challenged her to read the Bible because that is supposed to be our reference point.

❖

One night my daughter's friend, Bill, called me at a rather bad time, and he said, "Mr. Shapiro, I have a question for you."

I replied, "Can't it wait, Bill? I'm really busy." The urgency in his voice finally got my attention.

"Jesus is going to return soon, and I don't want to be left behind! I just want to ask you how I can become a Christian?" he implored frantically. I realized I wasn't so busy after all and explained to him God's plan for salvation.

After the divorce, I was struggling to pay my bills because of attorney fees and other debts I had to pay because all the credit was in my name. The Lord promises in Matthew 6:33 that if you seek His kingdom first, He will supply all your needs. I was way behind in my bills, and Christmas was fast approaching. I had only thirteen dollars left to buy presents. Incredibly, two days before Christmas, I received a check for over three thousand dollars from the post office. They had failed to give me the raise that I was supposed to have received, and this was back pay to correct it. I was elated! I had enough money to pay all my bills and plenty for gifts as well.

My coworkers had seen all the suffering that I'd been going through for some time and questioned how I could be so peaceful. That was a testimony to my Christian faith.

Ralph

When I started my job at the new post office, I met an extremely unique and obnoxious character. Ralph was big—over six feet tall and more than three hundred pounds. He was also very loud and crude, as well as extremely quick-witted. Nobody wanted to mess with him since he was a terrible bully.

There were thirty of us working in close quarters, so everyone could hear his booming voice. For the first six months, I was his primary target as all bullies need a victim. For such a rough character, he had a surprisingly good voice and often sang on the job.

When a song was playing on the radio one day, he changed the lyrics from "I don't care anymore" to "Morey has no hair anymore." No matter how hard I tried to defend myself from his tactics, he was too quick-witted for me.

But one day, he went too far and shouted, "Jews are no good! I hate them all. They've ruined our country." He was not only a bully but a white supremacist. Something rose up in me so quickly that I challenged him,

"I'm Jewish and one more word out of you, and I'll take care of you on the back dock!" I couldn't believe what I'd just said, as he was almost twice my size.

My friend said, "I'll bet on Morey. He's an athlete," adding fuel to the fire.

Unbelievably, the big brute then backed down and apologized to me and never harassed me again. Now, whenever he sees me, he acts like my best friend.

He later confessed to me, "I used to be the choir leader at church, but I lost my faith. You've proven to me that you're a true Christian."

CHAPTER ELEVEN

A Special Friendship

I was now forty years old, and I was still hoping to meet the right woman. I had been attending a Bible study group at a friend's house for several months. One week a beautiful young woman came to the meeting. She looked to be in her early twenties... much too young for me! But as we both continued to go to those meetings, we developed a friendship, and I learned she wasn't quite as young as I'd thought. She told me she was going to services at a Bible school about forty miles away.

I visited there and absolutely loved it, so we started riding together. We were still just friends, but I hoped for a deeper relationship. We had so much in common. We both loved to play tennis and attend Bible conferences together. She had all the qualities I desired to have in a wife: a nice personality, deep spirituality, and a love of fun and adventure. I prayed that someday she would see that we were perfect for each other, though she had expressed she just wanted a friendship.

Carol moved to a house on a lake nearby, and knowing my love for swimming told me, "Morey, you can come and swim anytime you want to." Little did she know that I would be there every day!

And little did I know that she'd been praying for God to bring her the right man to be her husband. In fact, after we'd been friends for about a year, God spoke to her clearly that I was the one. He had spoken that to me early on, but I was patiently waiting for her to see the light. After we dated several months, I asked her to marry me, and her reply was music to my ears.

Soon, I was in my own utopia married to the woman of my dreams and living in a house on a lake. It was wonderful beyond imagination.

❖

Bart

One of my coworkers, Laura, had a desire to learn about God. This led to a Bible study in her home, which I taught for about four years. Her husband, Don, attended the studies and, for the first year, didn't seem too interested. Then one week, he suddenly began to come alive spiritually. He became a born-again believer, and at least ten people were baptized and committed their lives to Christ through this group.

Laura's friend Jan had been attending the meetings and had a strong faith in God. She asked me, "Would you please come and pray for my father? He's been diagnosed with lymphoma." Her father had a reputation as a real tough guy. I was intimidated at first because I had never met him. I felt I had to say yes, but I made a few stipulations.

"I'm not going alone. You'll have to meet me outside his house." I demanded.

I arrived five minutes early, and it looked like no one was there. I was really upset. I waited several more minutes, but still, nobody arrived. I didn't see any cars around, and the house looked dark. Finally, I hesitantly walked to the door, feeling very uncomfortable. I knocked and was ushered in. To my astonishment, I found eight people sitting around a table waiting for me.

I was introduced to Bart and the rest of the group there. What I saw really alarmed me. Bart looked like death warmed over. He was very feeble, nothing like the fighter I'd heard about. He was resting both arms on the table, and it looked like he could barely hold his head up with his hands. He had lost seventy pounds and was like a living skeleton. My initial thought was that this man is going to die—maybe even within the next few days. I didn't have faith that he would be healed. I reasoned that the only thing to do was to lead him to salvation in Christ, so he would be ready to go to heaven soon.

When his daughter prepped me ahead of time for the visit, she had said, "He doesn't know anything about God, and he doesn't attend any church!" When I questioned him and offered to give him a Bible study, He replied,

"I already know everything about God!"

I was taken aback by his response, but I told him, "Let me share a little from God's Word." I started by telling him that there is an afterlife, and that he should prepare himself to make sure heaven would be his eternal home. I told him he needed to ask Jesus to forgive his sins and to come into his heart and make Him Lord and Savior, and he would have eternal life. I went home feeling a little discouraged but soon received a phone call asking me to come back the following week.

Bart and his wife Suzy informed me that they had both prayed and invited Christ into their hearts. They thanked me and desired to learn more about God. I took my wife with me this time, and we laid hands on Bart and prayed for healing, according to the Scriptures (James 5:14). For the next six months, we were invited to share the Gospel with them and their family and friends who made up the group.

The change we observed was truly amazing. Bart came alive and was not only receiving spiritual food, but we saw him at the Dairy Frost eating a banana split! He was putting on weight and looked healthy. He was healed of cancer. It wasn't because of our great faith, or even his own. I believe God honored his daughter's faith in performing that miracle.

Most doctors don't believe in miracles, and they demanded that he take a low dosage of chemotherapy. In the medical field, they believe that you are cancer-free if nothing comes back after five years. These events took place over twenty years ago, and Jan recently told me, "My father is still healthy; the cancer never returned!"

The Bible study, which was created to help Bart, led to the formation of a new study I was invited to lead in another home in that same area. Then Carol and I started a group at our house.

CHAPTER TWELVE

The Three Muslims

Getting back to the three Muslims. After a few hours of rambunctious debate, I felt I had come to an impasse with them. They didn't understand much about the Bible or the Koran. They just kept reiterating their conviction.

"You are what you're born!" This mindset held them captive; therefore, they weren't open to accepting my beliefs. I felt it was time to reveal my real identity to them. When I told them that I was raised in the Jewish faith and had converted to Christianity, they were stunned.

I believe there's a special key in sharing our faith, which varies with the different individuals we speak to. This was absolutely true in this case. Now I had their attention. All the reasoning in the world wouldn't convince them a bit, but my testimony of changing my religion was extremely impactful with them. I told them

I was now a Messianic Jew, one who believes that Jesus is the Messiah.

I didn't put any pressure on them to accept Christ. Often people need time to digest what they've heard and for God to prepare them to make that decision. I've heard it said that you must first win someone's heart and then they will listen to you. Jesus was the friend of sinners before He became their savior (Luke 7:34).

I visited them later in the week, not knowing what to expect. They warmly welcomed me and thanked me for the wonderful time they had at our home. They confided in me that they felt most Americans looked at them like they were terrorists because of 9/11. They said we viewed them differently, and they were happy to be our friends. They also asked me, "Why do you care about us so much?"

"I've found a great treasure, and I want to share it with you," I replied. Their response was encouraging, but when they said they wanted to come to our home Bible study, I almost fell over. The truth is, I had not actually invited them to come, though naturally, I was happy that they wanted to attend. Obviously, after our lengthy discussion, they were curious about it.

So, true to their word, they arrived at our home Saturday evening when we held our Bible study. Mel, who spoke little English, even brought his Muslim prayer beads with him. This was going to be an interesting night!

I never knew from week to week who was coming to the home meetings. Several women who lived in neighboring towns would come sporadically. Sometimes we had students and staff come all the way from the Bible school, where we'd been attending services. Some weeks we had over twenty and other weeks less than ten.

What an array of characters we met over the years. Most people were very teachable and pleasant, but there were a few who were a trial! A small number of men who came were obviously not there to learn but to try to teach and take over. These dominating personalities were definitely irritating.

That evening, we had a smaller group but at least one very strong personality. Pat, whose real name was Pasquale, was in his seventies but not a bit mellowed. He had grown up in Fascist Italy under Mussolini's reign. He and his family had lived in a Catholic neighborhood, though they were Protestant Christians. Therefore, they were strongly persecuted for their religious beliefs.

He told us the story of how, when his family would hold Bible studies in their home, they would gather around the dining table and always keep one hollowed-out loaf of bread at the ready in case of a police raid on their house. Bibles were illegal under Mussolini s reign. If they heard the police coming, they would quickly put the Bible they were using in the hollowed-out loaf to hide it from the authorities. He had come to America in the 1950s. Maybe because of his early suffering, he was exceptionally serious about his faith. He was passionately zealous but not terribly sensitive in his dealings with people of different religious backgrounds.

My nerves felt tense as I prepared for potential fireworks that night. There had already been a few times in the past, where I'd had to act as more of a referee than a Bible teacher! My wife says I have a very high people tolerance, which she admits she doesn't possess. Sometimes, I am maybe a little too tolerant or laid back in dealing with problem people. This may be due to my childhood, where craziness was the norm.

My mother-in-law, Barbara, who came to our home group for a long time, used to say that she didn't suffer fools gladly. She had a kind heart, though, and when one of the nuttier types went missing for several weeks, she wryly remarked, "I kind of miss his foolishness."

I introduced our Turkish friends to the rest of the group. Nick, the ringleader of the three, was loud and gregarious. He was intelligent and ambitious, looking for any way to make a fast buck in this land of opportunity that he loved.

Mike was more subdued and serious. He was here to learn English, as he worked toward his goal of becoming a veterinarian, a goal he shared with his roommate, Mel. Mel, as I mentioned, couldn't communicate with us since he spoke virtually no English yet. This, of course, made it hard to get to know him, but he was peaceful and friendly. In their native country, Turkey, about 99 percent of the population are Muslims.

I began to teach from the third chapter of the Gospel of John. I initially made the remark that John, who was Jesus' closest disciple, wrote the book. Nick immediately became agitated. "You mean Jesus didn't write the New Testament?" he interrupted.

"No," I said. "And Mohammed didn't write the Koran either!"

He was visibly upset at this revelation. I could see Pat was irritated, but thankfully he remained silent. I realized that most Christians from his era adhered to a strict protocol with any type of religious meeting; interrupting the speaker was certainly not a part of that. But this wasn't a church service, and I always looked for lots of participation in my Bible studies anyway.

I explained that all Scripture is inspired by God, according to 2 Timothy 3:16. I then proceeded to discuss

John 3:3. Many people struggle with the term born-again, which came straight out of the mouth of Jesus when He was talking to Nicodemus, a religious leader—Jesus replied, "Very truly I tell you, no one can see the kingdom of God unless they are born again" (John 3:3 NIV). A spiritual rebirth is a requirement of the Christian faith. Nick then blurted out loudly, "We believe in Jesus, but He is only a prophet, not the Son of God! Mohammed was the final prophet and, therefore, the greatest messenger of God!"

This was too much for Pat! He could hold back no longer. He angrily began to recount all the violent verses of the Koran and told the Muslims that they needed to repent and follow the true God. Oy Vey! This was going to be a long night. All I wanted was a peaceful Bible study, but with this bunch, it was turning into a nightmare! I had to calm the storm so that I could finish my chapter. Jesus was full of grace and truth, and this is the way to approach people. Grace is unconditional favor, and once you win somebody's heart, they will respond to truth.

By some miracle, I restored peace to the group and was able to finish the study without further interruptions! I know my wife, for one, was praying throughout that time. All of humanity falls short of God's glory, including Christians who are seeking to do God's will.

Pat, as I said, had a great zeal to serve God, though, like all of us, wasn't always sensitive to the Holy Spirit's leading.

I think, at times, the Lord may supernaturally intervene to protect those He is working to save. Does He put some spiritual earplugs on the seeker to keep them from hearing what shouldn't have been said? I don't know. But I know He is loving and merciful in nature, and He uses imperfect vessels to do His work on earth.

Still, when Mike later told me he'd like to go to church with us, I was astounded. Once again, I hadn't even extended an invitation to him. Mike and Mel also wanted us to tutor them in English and to continue our tennis matches. They kept us pretty busy for many months. Mike attended services with us for seven straight weeks. We were going to a small non-denominational church, which was very solid in Bible teaching. Mike really liked the pastor and appreciated the sermons. There was only one problem; like too many congregations these days, it was mainly a gray-headed population of believers.

Mike asked me, "Do only old people go to church in America?" I then took him to a large church, which was attended by loads of young people. Mike clapped his hands to the worship music and had a big smile on his face.

I had loaned Mike, the movie *Jesus of Nazareth*. He was deeply moved after viewing this video. He asked if he could keep it for a while. "Nick and Mel must see this film!" he said excitedly. "What was your favorite part?" I asked him. "The crucifixion and resurrection scenes," he answered without hesitation. The Koran says that it wasn't Jesus who died on the cross but someone who looked like him.

Everything had been going so smoothly with Mike. I guess I should have been prepared for spiritual warfare. When a person turns to Christ, he leaves the kingdom of this world, which is ruled by Satan to join God's kingdom. Therefore, the ruler of this world is not happy! Satan doesn't want to lose his lordship over any life, and he will fight to retain that mastery.

The following Sunday, we had planned to take Mike to church with us once again, but he had disappeared, and we couldn't locate him anywhere.

CHAPTER THIRTEEN

Becoming a Shepherd

My Wife

When I married Carol, I didn't realize how much healing I needed. God knew just what I needed when He brought her into my life.

I had lost my confidence and the vision the Lord had given me many years earlier. I had given up on being a pastor. I took after my father, who was a real pessimist. I was only forty-three, but I thought it was too late, and that I'd failed in achieving my calling. It's sad how negative thoughts and feelings can work on us to destroy our destiny. Carol is an idealist who always looks on the positive side of things.

She saw the gifts that God had given me in teaching and ministering to people and convinced me to pursue my dreams. My heart began to come alive again. When someone loses meaning and purpose in their life, their heart begins to die. My wife's gift of encouragement helped me to achieve my calling.

I was finally ordained as a minister in 1999. I had a strong desire to fulfill God's plan for my life. I believe everyone should seek the Lord's leading in finding any job, but in searching for a position as a pastor, it seems especially critical. God's will isn't a broad spectrum with a multitude of choices as the world sees man's path. The Scripture says, "But small is the gate and narrow the road that leads to life, and only a few find it" (Matthew 7:14 NIV). God doesn't always drop His plan specifically into our minds right away. Sometimes, He wants us to search it out. That's part of the growth process.

After I was ordained, I was eager to find opportunities to minister, and of course, I was hoping to find a full-time position as pastor of a church. I wasn't ordained into any denomination, though, so this was not necessarily an easy quest.

My wife said, "Let's pray. God will open doors." I thought she was a little too idealistic.

I said, "Do you think someone is just going to call and offer me a position?"

A few days later, the phone rang, and I was invited to interview for a pastorate in the Syracuse area. A pastor we had met at the Bible school was looking to plant a new church from his burgeoning congregation.

We visited the church and were well received. The only problem was the way this pastor was growing the church. He had bought into the seeker-friendly movement, which has been sweeping the nation for probably at least twenty years. We were appalled to see that the church was offering people coffee and doughnuts during the worship service. Whatever happened to coffee hour after or even before the service? God has called His servants to make disciples not build a spiritual Starbucks empire.

This minister, like me, had experienced a deep level of God's manifest presence in the past. The situation was dismaying to us. He also told us that there would be some strict guidelines to follow if we were to take the new church. He said we could only have six songs in a service, three of which must be hymns. Again, we were disturbed by these legalistic requirements. Carol and I were used to much freedom in the Spirit at the Bible school, where we had attended services for many years.

My heart was torn. I was sorely tempted to take the position, knowing that I might not receive any other offers. I had such a strong desire to begin to move in my calling after waiting so many years! But as I prayed about it, I realized I couldn't compromise my standards. Like so many situations in life, this was a test. God was testing my faithfulness to Him and His principles. I turned down the offer, and I went back to waiting and praying again.

To my surprise, another opportunity was presented to me in an unusual way. One of my relatives had visited a remote, rural congregation that was in need of a new minister. She suggested that I call them. I did, and I was invited to speak there.

When we arrived at this country church, Elder Joe firmly laid down the rules. "When you hear the fire whistle sound, you know it's time to wrap it up!" he admonished very seriously.

They obviously were not going to tolerate any long-winded preachers! This really wasn't an issue for me. I think that speaking too long is one of the worst mistakes a preacher can make and unfortunately a very common one.

Sure enough, as I made my closing remarks, I heard the loud blast of the fire whistle, and, as if on cue, I saw a big hound dog wander into the back of the sanctuary like he owned the place. At least he was quiet! Maybe this church was critter friendly. We just knew it wasn't the place for us.

Then I was informed that the small church I had attended for several years in Gloversville needed a pastor. That fellowship had been in decline for some time after the original founder had been driven out by a rebellious faction. It was a dying church in a dilapidated building. Nothing about the situation appealed to my wife, who has a degree in art and sophisticated taste. She found the place hard to stomach. It was a dark, windowless, shabby structure with rough, unfinished lumber on the inside walls. It had been thrown together decades earlier as an outlet store for the once vital glove industry in that city. But how could I refuse? I accepted the position as an interim pastor to test it out.

It seemed there were mouse traps everywhere in that church and for good reason. When I opened the door and turned on the lights before Bible study one night, I saw a slew of rodents scurry for cover. Maybe they were holding their own prayer meeting? And one Sunday morning in the middle of preaching my sermon, I saw a mouse run up the back wall. (No, not up the clock!)

From day one, we were frustrated there at every level. A new pastor wants to bring life and fresh vision to a congregation, but this paltry group was stuck in an incredibly deep rut. My mentor gave me some advice, "If you try to change things too quickly, they'll throw you out. First, win their hearts, and then there's a chance they will listen." But the board swiftly informed me that they loved my preaching, and that was all they wanted me to do. They opposed even the slightest and most obvious needs for change.

Carol was trying to find acceptance in her heart for the seedy sanctuary, but the decor was almost too tacky to be believed. A crude wooden ledge, which traced around all the raw lumber walls was covered with gaudy, orange candles. At the altar sat a gallon-sized, incredibly rusty paint can. When Carol suggested that the paint can be at least moved to the back table before the Christmas season, one man rushed to the front to make an almost tearful plea that it must remain where it was.

"It reminds us of when we collected pennies for Ethiopia years ago!" he gasped with a quavering voice. My wife bravely held her tongue, gritting her teeth. She wanted to shout, "Put it in the reliquary where it belongs!"

But the dysfunctional, little group clung to even more dangerous relics than that. In the middle of every service, they had a practice of praying for at least fifteen minutes, with each member taking a turn to drone on with their personal laundry lists of petitions. They worshiped their traditions and refused to consider any new ideas.

The tediousness of their rituals frustrated Carol so much that she would feel she needed to swim about fifty laps in her parent's pool after every service to calm herself down. They enjoyed my teaching but wanted no leadership, so I realized it was hopeless to try to revive this church. In fact, God told me to resign after nine months. I have seen that some churches literally need to die so that the Lord can raise up new life with new people. I won't deny that this was a discouraging chapter, though. I'm sure that's why God sent someone to give me a word of encouragement. A man prophesied over me, saying, "God is going to give you the desires of your heart, and you will be pastoring a church."

CHAPTER FOURTEEN

A Brand New Work

After I resigned from the interim pastorate, we continued to host a Bible study group in our home for a season. Then we felt God calling us to start a church in Gloversville. Our vision for this work came from Acts 2:42 (NLT), which specifies four basic foundations a church should be built upon. "All the believers devoted themselves to the apostles teaching, and to fellowship, and to sharing in meals (including The Lord's Supper) and to prayer." God quickened that scripture to us, emphasizing the need for balance in these areas. We have seen so many churches over the years that are out of balance in these four areas of the faith. For example, many groups have loads of doctrine and prayer but little or no fellowship. Others are basically social clubs without any solid teaching. When the early church practiced the discipline mentioned above, God abundantly blessed and increased the church.

We also believe that communion should be celebrated as a meal just as the early church did, instead of with dime-sized bits of crackers and sip sized cups of grape juice as most groups do today out of convenience, ignorance, or tradition. In the first century, the early church celebrated communion every Sunday night with a meal.

We were still idealists, of course, having had little experience in ministry up to that point. We had much to learn in dealing with people and spiritual warfare. Initially, we had presumed that our enthusiastic home group members would join us in launching the new work, but unfortunately, very few did. They loved the home meetings that moved in the freedom of the Holy Spirit but could not bring themselves to break away from their denominational churches on Sunday, which was ironic since their spiritual hunger was obviously what drew them to our meetings in the first place. This was a real handicap since, as we learned, you really need a solid core group to launch a healthy church.

We weren't prepared for the heavy spiritual warfare that bombarded us personally, as we stepped out in faith to pioneer this new work. Within a week, my wife had a car pull out abruptly in front of her, narrowly avoiding a head-on collision while I was rear-ended by a hit and run driver. Then at the very last minute, our chosen worship leader called and said he wouldn't be able to help us. I was comforted when a friend said: "If you are starting a new work and there's no warfare, I doubt it's from God."

We also felt ill-prepared for the type of group we found ourselves ministering to—mainly the homeless, alcoholics, drug addicts, and ex-convicts. I kept having dreams, which reflected Luke 4:18 (NKJV), "The spirit of the Lord is upon me, because He has anointed me to preach the Gospel to the poor, He has sent me to heal the brokenhearted, to proclaim liberty to the captives, and recovery of sight to the blind, to set at liberty those who are oppressed, to proclaim the acceptable year of the Lord." We had a church that was filled predominately with these types of hurting people. To say it was a difficult ministry would be a gross understatement. It was a huge challenge to love this bunch and lead them to salvation and healing in Christ.

We also had many different nationalities, and people of various religions attend our church. We had Muslims, Buddhists, and even a Palestinian visit. I thought it would be interesting to meet a Hindu next, so I prayed and asked God to send one to our church. The following Sunday, a new man arrived, and I greeted him. I asked, "What is your church background?"

He replied, "None. I'm a Hindu. I was just curious about your church." It was obvious that God had answered my prayer. What are the odds of that happening in a small town in upstate New York?

I shared a message on the virtues of Christ's life on earth. He thanked me since Christ is one of the three million god's Hindus worship. I remember reading the book, *The Death of a Guru* by Rabi R. Maharaj. His mother told him, "If you're ever in trouble, make sure you call on Jesus Christ to save you."

A few days later, as he was meditating, he opened his eyes and saw a large black cobra ready to strike him. He cried out to Jesus, and the snake departed. He became a Christian not long after that.

The Hindu religion is very confusing because there are so many gods they worship. Some are evil, and some are good. Hindus and Buddhists both believe in reincarnation. When we ministered to a Buddhist woman who had been abused by her husband, she made the remark, "I must have been abusive in my prior life for this to happen to me."

Many say all religions lead to God, but when you study each of them, you'll find many contradictions. God would have to be schizophrenic if He was saying all the radically diverse faiths lead to Him. Jesus said that He is the only way to God. "I am the way, the truth and the life. No man comes to the Father except through me" (John 14:6 NIV).

Headlines

When we first started our church, we asked the local newspaper to do a story on it. When they heard I was a Messianic Jew, they decided to interview me. They published a large photo of me teaching the congregation along with a fairly extensive article. I never dreamed of what an impact it would have on people, and I certainly wasn't prepared for the backlash it caused. My parents were quite disturbed since they didn't want the Jewish community to know about my conversion.

I walked into the YMCA and was immediately challenged by an old friend. "How could you betray your Jewish faith? The whole synagogue is talking about you, and they're very upset. We cannot be friends anymore because of your narrow thinking." I was stunned.

A few months afterward, the same guy approached me on crutches. He had fallen and broken his leg. When he saw how much I cared about his misfortune, his heart softened toward me. I was really surprised later when he asked me to explain what a Messianic Jew believes.

A Jewish professor at the local college, who'd read the article about me, told his students that I was the only Messianic Jew in the county. One of his students approached me and said, "You're famous." This professor had greatly influenced my wife's brother and inspired him to be a teacher. When her brother died, we had a service for him at our church. The professor came and heard me preach a message on God's mercy and compassion. After the service, he called a friend of mine, who was another former student, and said he couldn't understand why I thought God was so compassionate. Maybe this was because the Holocaust caused many Jewish people to question God's integrity and why He allowed such atrocities to take place. My friend told me this opened a door for him to share his faith with his former teacher.

I was also confronted at work one day by an elderly Jewish man. "Shapiro, what happened to you?" He was quite perturbed by what he had read. I invited him to lunch so we could talk.

Schlomo had an interesting history. He was born in Germany, and at the age of four, he and his father fled the country because of the Nazi persecution. His brother was supposed to leave the following day but was captured, and they never heard from him again. They arrived in Palestine in the 1930s.

He was an intelligent man and became a general in the Israeli army. He fought in the 1948 war after Israel became a nation. He told me all about the miracles he'd seen that saved them from destruction and credited that to God's divine intervention. He moved to the United States in 1965.

Schlomo and I became good friends. I listened to his heartbreaking accounts of losing a brother, a son, and his health. He was curious about my story, but not happy that I embraced Jesus as the Messiah. It amazes me how a person's life can be so full of tragedy, and yet not cry out to God. The last time I saw him before he passed away, he could barely walk and had lost all hope. I never heard whether he accepted Christ as Savior, but I know that it's possible even with someone's last breath.

Nursing Home

My wife and I had attended a prayer meeting for many years at an elderly lady's home, which was a real blessing. Her daughter and son-in-law were old friends. Sadly, this woman, whose name was Evelyn, fell and broke her hip and had to be confined to a nursing home.

She was dismayed to learn that the facility only offered one church service a month for the patients. God used this situation to speak to our hearts to start a couple more meetings there.

Initially, only a very small group attended, but as we began walking the halls and inviting many patients, the numbers increased considerably. My wife led worship, and I shared short teachings, but we found that the most important message we gave there was demonstrating God's love to the people. We saw how lonely those poor folks were and how desperately they needed a kind word and a warm handshake or hug. We greeted them all individually and watched their faces light up. We reached their hearts not because of our ability to preach or sing but by modeling Christ's love and compassion.

One week I heard the Lord speak to me to invite my mother to visit the nursing home with us. My mother had wanted nothing to do with my Christian faith, and I expected a very negative response from her. Truthfully, I didn't want to ask her at all. I had learned, however, not to contend with the Holy Spirit, so I obeyed God and invited her.

"I'd love to go with you!" she exclaimed.

After the first week, she said she wanted to go every time. She was already very elderly herself and bonded wonderfully with the patients. When I gave an invitation to receive Christ, my mother raised her hand. I was deeply moved. Another lady with large, bright blue eyes also requested prayer to receive Jesus into her life. A few days later, I opened the newspaper and read this woman's obituary. I know the angels were rejoicing to receive her into her heavenly home. Luke 15:10 (NIV) says, "In the same way, I tell you, there is rejoicing in the presence of the angels of God over one sinner who repents."

Bob

Nursing homes are, undoubtedly, some of the most depressing places on the face of the earth. My wife and I have spent a lot of time ministering in these institutions. But as sad as it is to see any person confined to that miserable existence, the most heartbreaking cases are those rare instances of the relatively young man or woman who has tragically been assigned to that fate. Naturally, a person in their forties or fifties who's a nursing home patient stands out like a sore thumb.

Bob was one of those horribly pathetic cases. He was only forty-nine when I met him. His story was so heart wrenching. He had a flat tire one day, and while changing it, he suffered a stroke and a heart attack. He became paralyzed on the left side of his body and had to be confined to a wheelchair. He was just 5'6" and weighed 348 pounds. He was also married with three young children. Within a year or two after his accident, his wife divorced him, and he rarely got to see his kids, which contributed greatly to his depressed state.

It's easy to judge others, which is a sin that Jesus condemned (Matthew 7:1). Why would someone let their weight get so out of control and put themselves in physical danger due to their obesity? It was obviously a case where food addiction became just as deadly as alcohol or drugs. I've interviewed many alcoholics and drug addicts, and I have found they're generally all running from traumatic experiences.

As I got to know Bob, one day he told me the rest of his story. "I never knew my father; my mother was a drug addict. When I was eight years old, she came home one night and told me to sleep on the floor so she could have the couch. She didn't wake up the next morning, and when I tried to rouse her, there was no response. She was dead, and I was left an orphan." There were clearly deep, longstanding, emotional wounds in his heart.

He wanted to come to our church, and I was glad to oblige him. On the way, he asked if we could stop and pick up his kids and bring them to church as well. We wanted to help him in any way we could. He gave his heart to Jesus and found peace. Then he asked to be baptized. I believe in full immersion baptism, which is the scriptural method, but it wasn't possible with Bob, so I just sprayed him down with a garden hose. He was okay with that, and he rejoiced in his newfound faith.

A Sticky Situation

It was a scorching day in July. It must have been at least ninety degrees when I left to go to a funeral for my friend Don's father. I was running a little late, and when I arrived at the church, I didn't see any seats available at first glance as I quickly surveyed the scene. Then I noticed one empty pew in the front row on the far right-hand side. It wouldn't have been my first choice by a long shot, but I was just thankful to find any seat at that point. So, after greeting my friend and his family and offering condolences, I made my way to the vacant pew feeling a little self-conscious. This was a very old church building, and there was no air conditioning, so I was already sweating profusely in my suit and tie. I plopped down and mopped my brow, as I prepared to endure the sweltering service.

We were gathered to honor the dead, but by the end, we all felt like we were dying of the heat in there. When it was over, I couldn't wait to get back to my air-conditioned car! But as I was about to stand up, I had the horrifying realization that I couldn't move. I was stuck! It literally felt like I was glued to the pew!

Terror gripped me as I contemplated possible outcomes. I'm sure my already overheated complexion turned several shades brighter as I considered the embarrassment of ripping my pants in the process of getting up. What were my options? Call for help? How humiliating would that be! I desperately started eyeing the choir robes the singers in the front were wearing. Would they come to my aid? And what was going on here? I guessed that they must have just revarnished the pew. (Maybe even earlier that day!) I shifted my position a bit and tested the waters. Perhaps if I moved ever so slowly? So, I began to peel my pants little by little an inch at a time from the pew. After what seemed like an eternity, I was free! Thank the Lord! I reminded myself that it would be undignified for any adult, much less an ordained minister, to run out of the church. So, I tried to stay calm and paced myself as I made for the door hoping that no one had noticed my predicament.

I thought I had escaped unscathed until I reached home and heard my wife gasp, "What's all that brown on the back of your pants?" She obviously had her own ideas! When I explained, she doubled over laughing. We have learned through the years that almost anything can happen in church and often does.

CHAPTER FIFTEEN

Forgiveness

It took me many years to learn to forgive others. It seemed unfair to have to forgive someone who chose to hurt me. But as one Christian writer pointed out, "Forgiveness is not about accepting or excusing someone's behavior. (God will judge them for that.) It's about letting go and preventing their behavior from destroying our own hearts" (Woldt 2017). Matthew 6:14–15 (NIV) says, "For if you forgive other people when they sin against you, your heavenly Father will also forgive you. But if you do not forgive others their sins, your Father will not forgive your sins." And in Ephesians 4:32 (NIV), it says, "Be kind and compassionate to one another, forgiving each other, just as in Christ God forgave you."

What I didn't comprehend years ago and what most Christians don't realize is that harboring unforgiveness or bitterness can even cause us serious, physical problems as well as emotional issues. When I was thirty-four, I went to the doctor with a bad knee injury. He took x-rays, and when the x-rays came back, he pointed out all the little dots on the inside of my knee. "You have the worst case of arthritis I've ever seen in such a young man. In twenty-five years, I doubt you will be walking!" he predicted gravely.

I knew I had serious problems with my knee, but this was devastating! At that time, I didn't understand spiritual warfare and that there can be spiritual roots to diseases such as sin in our lives. Unforgiveness, especially, is a poison to our entire system. God showed me that I had some key people I needed to forgive. I had allowed a lot of hatred and resentment to grow in my heart toward these individuals.

Though they had terribly wronged me, God showed me that I needed to let the offenses go. I did, and it's been thirty-four years since I received that doctor's dire prognosis, and thank the Lord, I am not having any problem walking. I am still very active and disciplined with exercising.

For a long time, I wondered why I was healed from arthritis. I had tried to keep a positive attitude, and I always exercised rigorously. Now I understand the key was forgiving those who had hurt me. I had always held everything inside and pretended I was fine, but I had a lot of bitterness in my heart toward several people. One of those people was my father.

There was a much deeper void in my childhood that went way beyond the total lack of discipline and practical life training that handicapped me in so many ways. Rejection by anyone can be painful, but rejection by a parent can cause profound wounding to the depths of a child's being. My father rejected me from an early age, and I still don't understand the reason why. It may have been the fact that my mother favored me, inciting a type of jealousy in him.

My parents both committed the unpardonable sin in parenting: favoritism. It seemed ironic that three of the six children resembled my father with olive skin and dark hair, while the other three (including me) had fair skin and light hair like my mother. My father tended to favor the ones that looked like him, and my mother, conversely, was partial to the kids who took after her. It almost seemed to be a game between them.

Every son especially wants and need's his father's love and acceptance. I felt terrible when it seemed I could do nothing right in my father's eyes. I brought home my report card from junior high school with a grade of ninety-six in math, with the rest of my grades being just average. He took one look at the marks and proclaimed that the only job I'd ever be able to get would be that of a garbage collector! I was crushed at the age of thirteen. My father hardly ever spoke to me, and when he did, all I ever heard was judgment or criticism. I lived with the pain of his rejection for over thirty years. I was always looking for a father figure to replace him in a teacher, coach, or coworker. I had a lot of anger in my heart toward my Dad, but I didn't realize it.

It was especially hurtful as an adult to call him and hear him sound really excited to hear my voice as he responded, "Jeffrey, it's so good to hear from you!" and then observe the let down when I told him it was me and not my brother.

When I was thirty-seven, I visited him at his new home in San Diego. He was seventy-five then, and I saw him in a new light as he was starting to show signs of aging. I made a decision I know God put in my heart—to forgive him. Once I had let go of all the pain and rejection, I felt like a huge burden was lifted from me. It brought tremendous peace and healing to my life even though his behavior didn't change.

When I finally forgave him and a few others who had deeply hurt me, the healing process began. Not only was my heart cleansed, but the arthritis completely disappeared. In my case, the arthritis came from unforgiveness, and I know many others have also experienced the same phenomenon.

In order to forgive others as Christ forgave us, we need to understand the great sacrifice He made for us.

He took our place on the cross and died for all of our sins. 2 Corinthians 5:21 (NLT) states, "For God made Christ, who never sinned, to be the offering for our sin, so that we could be made right with God through Christ." As we understand and experience God's forgiveness for us, something we didn't deserve, we should learn to forgive others.

MORRIS AARON SHAPIRO

CHAPTER SIXTEEN

Ministry

Steve

Steve was a brilliant man. He was an inventor, an engineer, and a retired major from the Air Force. He was in his early seventies when I met him. Steve was selling his invention online, and he and his wife, Theresa, would come to the post office almost every day to mail out packages of their product. That's how I got to know them. We hit it off so well that they started inviting us over for meals. What struck me most about Steve was his honesty. There wasn't an ounce of phoniness in him. He was a man of tremendous character, and I enjoyed visiting with him.

Theresa was very interested in religion. She was brought up Catholic and had a brother who was a priest and a sister who was a nun. She began attending services at our church and was deeply concerned about her husband's spiritual and physical condition. He had such bad osteoarthritis he could hardly walk.

Being very intellectual, Steve had trouble with Christianity because he couldn't logically figure God out. I shared with him about the historical accuracy of the Bible and all the prophecies that were fulfilled.

He said, "I'm an agnostic, and only ten percent of me believes in God."

We had an evangelist come to our church who had the gift of healing. Theresa persuaded Steve to come to the service, which I'm sure wasn't easy. The evangelist called all who wanted healing to come forward.

"I just wanna get the heck out of here! Please help me to the car!" Steve pleaded.

But Theresa would have none of it! She practically dragged him to the front of the church. It was obviously excruciating for Steve to hobble down to the altar, and it was hard for me to see him labor with every step he took.

Watching Steve and the healing evangelist interact was like watching a comedy show. God gave the evangelist, who'd never met Steve, a word of knowledge about him right away. He then aggressively challenged Steve with, "Who haven't you forgiven?"

Steve shouted back, "I'll never forgive him!"

"Then you're going to hell!" the evangelist roughly admonished.

"I am not," retorted Steve.

"The Bible says if you don't forgive others, God won't forgive you! Why don't you ask God to help you forgive your brother?"

Steve finally consented and was prayed for. When the minister laid hands on Steve, he was instantly healed and left the meeting walking perfectly normally. He remained pain-free for weeks. What joy! But unfortunately, Steve still harbored a grudge against his brother and hadn't yet given his heart to Christ. Consequently, after walking around pain-free for three weeks, the arthritis came back, and he could hardly move again.

Steve and I would have friendly debates all the time.

"How could you watch *The Passion of the Christ* five times?" I asked. Watching that movie once was enough for me. Steve was still an agnostic and would often tell me, "I just want to die."

I would always counter with, "God is not done with you yet!"

As the years went by, he became much worse physically. He was a large man, and Theresa, being extremely petite, could no longer take care of him at home. He had to go in a nursing home, which was extremely depressing, and his spirit plummeted. Steve was now in his eighties, and he sadly told me, "All my friends have either died or moved away."

I then recruited my buddies, Paul and Ben, who are zealous Christians, to help visit Steve. We would also take him to the movies and out to dinner at times. The four of us were riding in the car and talking about God when I asked Steve, "How do you like riding around with three Jesus freaks?"

"You guys certainly like to talk about the Bible," he responded in his calm voice. Steve finally invited the Lord into his heart two weeks before he passed away. He was won over not by debates but by love. His wife and his new Christian friends, who continually visited him, helped him to see the light. I look forward to a reunion with him in heaven someday.

Justin

One of my favorite converts is a man from the Philippines, whose name is Justin. He was invited to our Bible study by a friend, which is usually the way new people join these groups. The Filipino culture is warm and friendly, and Justin embodies these traits along with many other fine qualities.

At one of our meetings, we asked him if he'd ever been born-again spiritually. He told us that in his country, you had to join a club to experience that. I said, "Let me read you, John 3:16. 'For God so loved the world that he gave his only begotten Son, that whosoever believeth in Him should not perish, but have everlasting life'" (KJV). "Show me where it says you have to join a club!" He immediately prayed to receive Christ as his savior and was filled with abundant joy. He began reading the Scriptures and soon asked me if I would baptize him. I was only too happy to do so. We planned a date for the following week at a church picnic.

Justin had always been extremely popular, and like many foreign-born residents, had a large circle of friends from his homeland who had also immigrated to the U.S. It was easy to see that this was a vitally important connection for him and understandably so. Being new in a strange country could be a difficult adjustment for anyone, thus having the fraternity of one's own culture had to be a great comfort.

We looked forward to the picnic, which was an annual event at one of the neighboring churches we were close to. Many of Justin's Filipino friends came and witnessed his baptism. Justin was beaming with joy and excitement. It was a wonderful day for him.

The following week, though, he came to me with a heavy heart, and his countenance was downcast. He told me that many of his Filipino friends were now avoiding him, and He couldn't understand why.

When one of them came into the post office, I clearly got the message. "Justin has Morey's religion now!"

was what I heard spoken derisively. I tried to explain to his friend that it wasn't "my religion," but that it came straight from the Bible.

Catholicism is the dominant religion in the Philippines; eighty-six percent of the population professes that faith (Lipka 2015). One of the seven sacraments Catholics believe in is baptism, which they teach takes away the original sin inherited from Adam. Most have been baptized as infants. This had been the case with Justin. I think his friends felt he had rejected their common heritage and beliefs and were offended by that. I think that they may have been concerned that we represented some kind of cult. Many Catholics have never read the Bible and, therefore, don't understand the basis for Protestant beliefs or even much of their own doctrine.

Later I read 2 Timothy 3:12 (NIV) to Justin. "In fact, everyone who wants to live a godly life in Christ Jesus will be persecuted." The Scriptures also teach us to, "Rejoice and be exceedingly glad: for great is your reward heaven: for so persecuted they the prophets which were before you" (Matthew 5:12 KJV; Matthew 5:11, 13). Yes, this was a clear example of those verses in action. And though the Bible teaches that we as believers are blessed to receive persecution, it's not always easy to take, especially when it involves rejection by close friends or family members.

Justin continued to follow Christ despite the pain of that experience, and thankfully over time, many of those friends became reconciled to him and his new-found faith. A few even visited our church.

Justin became one of my most loyal church members and disciples. I will always cherish his friendship and remember his faithfulness. If I could choose twelve disciples to change a city, he would be at the top of the list.

Sandy

Sandy and his wife came to visit our church one week, and they ended up staying for three years despite having to drive an hour each way. They were tired of being spectators in another church. They were Bible school graduates, who were looking to minister to the Body of Christ (the church). So, we put them to work.

Sandy had quite an amazing story. He idolized his father as a young boy; they did everything together. This came to an abrupt and heartbreaking end, however, when his parents divorced, and his dad basically dropped out of his life. The emotional turmoil came to a head when he was fifteen, and he ran away from home. Somehow, he managed to find employment at this young age and became self-sufficient.

One day as he was crossing a busy street, he was hit by a truck and propelled into a concrete wall. He felt his spirit leave his body, and he had the sensation that he was drowning. Many people were trying to save him, but all their frantic attempts were futile. He knew he was headed for hell when suddenly, Jesus reached out and saved him!

He had not become a Christian up to this point, and interestingly, he did not immediately accept Christ after this profound experience.

When he came back to earth, spiritually speaking, he was in excruciating pain having so many horrific injuries—a broken leg, ruptured spleen, head injuries, and fractured ribs, just to mention a few. It was a miracle he survived. The road to recovery was long and arduous.

One day, out of boredom, he flipped on a Christian radio program. As he listened to the Gospel message, a light went on in his heart and mind. He gave his life to Jesus on the spot. Ironically, God also gave him a gift of healing, which the Bible describes in 1 Corinthians 12:9. Any believer in Christ can pray for the sick and see them healed by the power of God, but not everyone has this special anointing, which is the gift of healing. I believe Sandy was chosen to receive this gift because he learned to have compassion for the afflicted due to all the personal suffering he endured.

> *Praise be to the God and Father of our Lord Je-*
> *sus Christ, the Father of compassion and the God of*
> *all comfort, who comforts us in all our troubles, so*
> *that we can comfort those in any trouble with the*
> *comfort we ourselves receive from God.*
> (2 Corinthians 1:3–4 NIV)

The word of knowledge, another spiritual gift, often accompanies the gift of healing. At one Bible study, Sandy asked if he could share a word the Lord had given him. I willingly gave him the green light.

"Somebody here has been having severe sinus problems for a long time. The Lord is going to heal you now," he proclaimed. I looked around. I knew most everyone in this small congregation well, and I hadn't heard of anyone with this ailment. But there was one new woman visiting that day, and sure enough, she acknowledged that she fit the description. She was instantly healed of all her sinus troubles, and she was thrilled.

God also healed another man who couldn't straighten his arm. It was turned inward toward his chest. He was fired from his job because he was unable to use this arm. Not many days after receiving prayer, I saw him walking down the street, swinging both arms freely. It was really exciting to see God's miraculous power at work in our midst.

The church is a body of believers and should allow people to move in their gifts. No pastor should be a one-man show. 1 Corinthians 14:26 (NIV) says, "What then shall we say, brothers and sisters? When you come together, each of you has a hymn, or a word of instruction, a revelation, a tongue, or an interpretation. Everything must be done so that the church may be built up." The church should not make spectators but participants.

Jon

One week a young man appeared at our church just bursting with enthusiasm. Jon was in his mid-twenties, and he was fresh out of prison, having served time for selling drugs. He'd had a jailhouse conversion, which seemed to be rock solid. He was living in a halfway house for addicts and was passionate about serving Christ. He had a tremendous outgoing personality, and everyone liked him.

I spent a lot of time mentoring Jon as did another local pastor, and he was making great progress. He came to our church services and Bible studies for two straight years and was living uprightly all that time. He was bright and talented and donated his time to build a wheelchair ramp onto our house, so Carol's mother could visit.

We warned him of the danger of backsliding. So many addicts unfortunately do. But Jon didn't think that could happen to him. Proverbs 16:18 (KJV) says, "Pride goeth before destruction, and a haughty spirit before a fall." 1 Corinthians 10:12 (NKJV) states, "Therefore, let him who thinks he stands take heed lest he fall." I would also like to add that anyone who thinks he could never fall most likely will.

And sadly, Jon did. It was exceedingly painful to watch, especially since he ended up in prison once again. He was like a son to me, and this broke my heart. What triggered his downfall, you may ask? I'd say that it was a classic case of his getting involved with the wrong crowd, specifically the wrong woman.

The Bible gives serious guidelines when it comes to our relationship with the opposite sex. These are for our protection and should be strictly adhered to. We're commanded not to be unequally yoked together with unbelievers (2 Corinthians 6:14). This refers to dating, marriage, and even business partnerships.

Jon wrote me eloquent letters from prison full of contrition and pathos. There is always hope for anyone to recover if they will sincerely turn to God for help. God doesn't ever give up on anyone, and neither should we.

I had great expectations for him when he was released. I hate to say it, but maybe Jon was released too soon! It seems to be easier for some to be spiritual in prison, where the temptation is minimal and there's a secure structure for their lives. He'd also been given much leniency for each period of incarceration.

When he got out this time, he quickly fell back into his old habits and we witnessed a complete personality change when he again became a drug user. My wife read threatening emails he sent to a female church member. He was no longer in control of his life; the drugs had taken over.

Even scarier was the fact that in his good years with us, we had introduced him to several elderly friends who hired him to paint their houses and do odd jobs. Now we felt that we had to contact those people and warn them to steer clear of Jon, desperately hoping Jon would stay away from them and their properties.

This raises the issue of how involved ministers and church members should get with drug addicts. We knew a young couple with an outreach ministry to recovering addicts who had a terrible trial in this area. They had unwisely let a former addict, who like Jon, had been clean for a fairly long period of time, move into their home with them and their little children. This became a dangerous scenario when the man fell back into addiction.

The church needs to reach out to these people, but much caution should be employed. Jon was sentenced to prison for the third time. We continue to pray for him that he will turn back to the Lord and overcome his bondage to sin.

A Mysterious Visitor

We never knew who was going to visit our church. One Sunday, a very strange character walked through the door. He was wearing jeans and a muscle shirt and looked awfully angry. He acted extremely paranoid, as he wouldn't sit near anybody or even tell us his name.

We had a small crowd that Sunday, which included another visitor who confessed he was straight out of prison and had been the largest drug dealer in the county. As I surveyed the rest of the people there, I realized that one of our members had also been released from jail recently. It was a rough bunch to be sure!

We felt led by the Holy Spirit to change our whole plan for church that day. A traditional church service wasn't going to get through to this crowd. I changed my message to Luke 4:18 (KJV), where Jesus says, "The Spirit of the Lord is upon me, because he hath anointed to preach the gospel to the poor, he hath sent me to heal the broken hearted and to preach deliverance to the captives, recovering of sight to the blind, to set at liberty them that are bruised." There was no guarantee that any of these people would come back to our church again, so I wanted to tell them about the love of God.

At first, the terribly troubled young man was interrupting the sermon and pacing around like a caged animal. We found that many unchurched people like him were used to AA meetings, where there was mainly group discussion. I told him he could ask questions at the end—but no more interruptions. As I continued to speak, I could see that the young fellow became more relaxed. He eventually even sat down.

After the service, he came up to me, shook my hand, and thanked me for not judging him. He also told me he enjoyed the message! He never did tell me his name, but he did say that when he was in prison, they called him "Psycho" because he liked to hurt people.

I shared this story with a friend, and he said, "Your church is too dangerous for me!"

A Tale of Two Churches

During one phase of our development, our church rented space at the local YWCA to hold services. Another church rented a room in the same building. The only thing separating the congregations was a shared kitchen.

The two churches were as different as night and day. We were charismatic and non-denominational. They had Baptist origins but had mutated into something very far afield from their conservative roots. Despite the radical differences in our doctrines, there was peace between us, that is, until God moved one chess piece.

That Sunday morning, I was approached by an old high school friend. Sidney was a super conservative Christian, who had been attending the other church until he crossed the invisible border fence to seek asylum with me. He was incredibly agitated as he waved his Bible in the air.

"Do you believe this book?" he questioned emphatically.

"I certainly do," I responded.

He pointed toward his church across the hall and said, "My pastor doesn't believe the Bible anymore. I'm leaving his fellowship. Can I come to your church?"

"Sure," I replied. What else could I say?

"Why did your pastor lose his faith?" I questioned him.

He was asked to leave the Baptist denomination due to being alone with a woman he was counseling. They had warned him to stay away from the appearance of evil (Thessalonians 5:22). He became bitter and decided that the Bible wasn't reliable anymore. Sidney was disgusted and frustrated.

This type of scenario is becoming far too common these days. When this happens in a church, the minister often tries to take the congregation down with him. When my friend's pastor left his denomination, he went rogue and convinced many innocent souls to follow him down the wrong path. When he heard that Sidney had left his fellowship to join our group, he was furious! The heat was definitely turned up in the kitchen we shared. He cornered me there and demanded I come to a meeting with him and one of his elders.

He was tremendously angry as he confronted me.

"You're a sheep stealer!" he railed. "What you're doing is unethical. You should be ashamed of yourself," he shouted loudly.

"If you still believed in the Bible, Sidney never would have left your church," I calmly countered. "Besides, it was entirely his own decision. I did nothing to sway him," I reproved. I knew the real reason this backslidden cleric was so irate, though. It was because Sidney was a generous giver who practiced tithing (giving ten percent or more of his income to the church).

Jesus warned His disciples that there would be many false teachers who would lead multitudes astray. Where is Satan going to try to deceive God's people? Predominantly in the church, of course. That's why we are admonished to test the spirits and to beware of wolves in sheep's clothing (1 John 4:1; Matthew 7:15). Jesus said in the end times, even the elect could fall into deception.

> *For false messiahs and false prophets will appear and perform great signs and wonders to deceive, if possible, even the elect.*
> (Matthew 24:24 NIV)

Jesus also said, "You shall know them by their fruits..." (Matthew 7:20 NKJV). This refers to their deeds or behavior.

Guardian Angels

Every good parent wants to save their children from dangerous situations, but occasionally circumstances render that impossible. The Bible teaches that we all have angels watching over us (Psalm 91:11). Jesus mentioned that all youngsters have their own guardian angels (Matthew 18:10).

My sister Marsha shared a touching testimony with me, which illustrates this fact. Her son, who was eight years old, was taking a nap when she left to go grocery shopping. Her husband didn't realize she had left, so he also departed, leaving their son alone.

While they were gone, a huge fire broke out on their street, and many houses were burned to the ground. The fire was rapidly moving toward their residence when a neighbor saw two men on the roof hosing down their house. The fire destroyed all the homes around them, but theirs was untouched. They would have lost their son and the house if it wasn't for the two men on the roof.

She and her husband had no idea who the two men were. They disappeared quickly, and nobody could trace their origin. My sister believes they were angels. The Bible says, "God will command His angels concerning you to guard you in all your ways" (Psalm 91:11 NIV).

❖

My daughter, Jessica, also shared a story of how God protected her son, Christian. She was doing laundry in the basement when suddenly her two-year-old son opened the cellar door and thought he could jump down to her. She was in total terror when she saw him leap. He was coming down headfirst when, suddenly, something turned him, and he flipped over and landed on his feet. She had no explanation for this miracle but then realized it must have been his guardian angel who rescued him.

CHAPTER SEVENTEEN

Hearing God's Voice

One of the most exciting aspects of having a relationship with Christ is learning to hear His Voice. It is a learning process, and though I've often missed it by failing to listen to Him and going my own way, I've had some very exceptional experiences when I know I've clearly heard Him speak to me.

Jesus encouraged His disciples to get alone with the Father each day to receive guidance. We need to get away from distractions so that we can hear God's voice. The Lord's prayer in Mathew 6:9–13, teaches us how to pray. It's meant to be a model to train us, not something we mindlessly recite. Our focus should be on God, not ourselves. When we want God's will and His kingdom, it opens the heavens for God to speak to us. We should start each day in prayer, asking God for wisdom and direction so we can impact the world around us.

In the following accounts, I will relate several stories of hearing God speak to me in various situations and a few cases where I missed His leading.

Barbara

One interesting person I met at the post office was Barbara. She was a Buddhist professor from China who was teaching religious studies at a state college nearby. I had a habit of loaning out Christian DVDs and books to customers I knew who were searching for God. She was right behind one of these customers as she stood in line one day and saw me passing out DVDs. I was taken aback when she asked, "Do you have any DVDs to loan to me?" I "just happened" to have two movies about Chinese Christians, which I loaned to her. She was deeply moved after viewing them and thanked me profusely. I saw her not long afterward at the Christian bookstore ordering more materials.

Every morning before I left for work, I would pray and seek to hear God's Voice. One day the Lord spoke to me to take the book, *The Heavenly Man* by Brother Yun and give it to Barbara. *The Heavenly Man* is a true story of a Christian who lived in communist China. China only allows Christians to attend government-approved churches. Ministers cannot preach anything without government approval, so many Chinese Christians hold church services in their homes. These house churches are considered illegal, and many have been arrested and sent to prison for this so-called crime. This is one man's testimony of suffering for his faith and the astonishing miracles God performed in his life.

We all have a selfish, fleshly nature, and while I was glad to loan out most of my books, I didn't like to give too many away. They are some of my most treasured possessions, and that book is one of my all-time favorites. So, I said, "Okay, Lord, I'll loan it to her."

Sure enough, Barbara was my first customer of the day. When I offered to loan her that book, she looked disappointed. "I am leaving for China today and never coming back," she professed. I was immediately convicted of my covetousness.

"God told me to give you this book, and I want you to have it," I relented. She beamed with pleasure and thanked me warmly.

This was a lesson to me of how specifically God wants to communicate with us. Our test is whether we choose to listen and obey Him.

Scientist

I was on my way to visit my parents. They had moved to California after my father retired. It was going to be a long flight, and I prayed for the Lord to put someone interesting next to me to talk to. He answered that prayer in an exceptional manner.

My seatmate introduced himself to me. He told me he was a scientist. That was certainly interesting! This was obviously not your average Joe. We began a friendly conversation. I was curious to know what he believed about God. So, I posed three questions.

"Do you believe in God?" "Do you believe He is a personal God? And, if so, has He revealed a purpose and plan for mankind?"

He answered, "Yes, I believe there is a God who created the universe, but no, I don't believe He is personal or can be known."

He was like Benjamin Franklin and many of America's founding fathers, who were deists believing in a divine creator but not a God who can be personally known by mankind. We talked for three solid hours, which I found very stimulating. He was a great intellectual, and at first, I was a little intimidated since I'd never studied much science. But that didn't matter because I had the Holy Spirit's help. We need to be sensitive to the Spirit of God in every situation. With a word from Him, you can reach into the depths of someone's heart.

"Why don't you pray and ask God to reveal Himself to you." I gently challenged him. His response shocked me. He threw up his hands and said, "No, I'm afraid! He might tell me something bad!"

"The God I know is full of love." I quoted 1 John 4:18 (NIV), "There is no fear in love, but perfect love drives out all fear, because fear has to do with punishment. The one who fears is not made perfect in love."

He was visibly touched, and as our flight ended, he shook my hand and said, "Thank you for sharing with me. I never comprehended God in that way before." This illustrates that God will give us wisdom and a word that will touch someone's heart (Isaiah 50:4).

The Lost Keys

Most people only seek God's guidance (if they do at all) when it comes to the major issues of life. But God desires to give us wisdom and direction in every area, even in the smallest matters.

I was put in charge of the stamp machine in the post office lobby. This probably doesn't sound like a big deal, but the inventory of stamps in the machine was worth thousands of dollars. I was given a set of keys for it and admonished to use extreme caution since it was the only set they had.

I tried to be careful always putting the keys in my pocket after I restocked the machine, but one day I noticed they were missing. At first, I assumed that they would turn up, but after a week of frantic searching, they were still nowhere to be found. I had tried to retrace my steps thoroughly, checking all the inside and outside areas of the building. I had looked all over the parking lot, and everywhere I'd ever put my foot down in the vicinity.

I dreaded having to tell the postmaster, but I knew that I would soon be forced to make that awful confession. One day, I had a divine inspiration. I finally thought of praying and asking for God's help in finding the keys.

When I arrived at work early that morning, there was about three inches of fresh snow on the ground. The plow had not been through yet. As I got out of my car and started toward the building, I heard the Holy Spirit speak to me in that small, inward voice. He impressed upon me that I should walk around a truck that was about fifty feet away. I started to the left, but He told me to go to the right. When I did so, my eyes fell upon a faint gleam of metal sticking out of the snow. I could hardly believe my eyes; I'd found the keys! What were the odds of me spotting them, especially when they were buried in the snow? Only the all-knowing Heavenly Father knew exactly where they were. It reminded me of Isaiah 30:21(NIV), "Whether you turn to the right or to the left, your ears will hear a voice behind you, saying, 'This is the way: walk in it.'"

Then I remembered the parable of the lost coin in the Bible, thinking that woman had prayed as I did. It taught me a valuable lesson. I'm sure, most of the time, we don't hear God's voice simply because we fail to pray and ask for His direction.

In Matthew 7:7 (KJV), Jesus told His disciples, "Ask, and it shall be given you; seek, and ye shall find; knock, and it shall be opened unto you." As we learn to listen to God in the little things, I believe He will train us to hear in greater matters.

A Strange Dream

> *And it shall come to pass in the last days, says God, That I will pour out of My Spirit on all flesh, Your sons and daughters shall prophecy, Your young men shall see visions, Your old men shall dream dreams.*
>
> (Acts 2:17 NKJV)

Many years ago, I had a dream about my friend Greg's youngest daughter, who was then about eight years old. I saw her walking down the street not far from their home when suddenly she was abducted by a very evil-looking woman. The woman's face was clearly and strongly imprinted on my mind. It gave me an eerie feeling. At first, I was hesitant to tell Greg about this, uncertain of the source of the dream. I went to the mall the next day and heard over the loudspeaker that a five-year-old child was missing. I immediately thought of Greg's daughter and the dream.

The following day I drove to Captain Video to rent a movie. The store was just a couple of blocks from Greg's house. I pulled in the lot and parked my car. I looked out the window and saw a woman in a nearby car staring at me. She had a terrible look in her eyes. I was shocked when I realized that it was the same woman I'd seen in my dream—the one who had kidnapped my friend's daughter. This was my third sign. I was now thoroughly convinced that I had heard from God and that He wanted me to warn my friend. Greg listened carefully when I told him about my dream, and the other signs God had revealed to me.

He thanked me and said, "I've been sending my daughter to that store regularly to return videos. I won't let her go there alone anymore." He also followed her down the street one day and realized how easy it would be for someone to abduct her. He and his wife were extremely vigilant in watching over their little girl, and thankfully she never fell into any danger. Satan's plans were thwarted.

This is one scriptural function of dreams, to warn God's people of potentially hazardous situations. The wise men were warned in a dream not to return to Herod to protect the infant Jesus from his murderous design (Matthew 2:12). Joseph was warned in a dream to take Mary and Jesus down into Egypt to avoid the death warrant Herod had placed on all children two years old and younger (Matthew 2:13).

We need to listen to God at all times and be super sensitive to His Spirit. There can be serious consequences if we don't obey a word from God: whether it's a dream, vision, or prophetic word.

Joseph

We were getting ready to take a train to New York City and had just paid to park our car at the station in Poughkeepsie. God was trying to get our attention as we noticed a remarkably tall African man who was struggling with a parking meter there. We offered a bit of help, which he gladly received. This opened the door to a friendly conversation. He had such a warm spirit that we invited him to sit with us on the train. The odd thing was that he looked somehow vaguely familiar, though we knew we had certainly never met him before.

His name was Joseph, and he told us he was from South Sudan. He proceeded to tell us his story. "My people are Christians, and about ten years ago, my village was attacked by a Muslim army from the north. They destroyed my village and so many more in South Sudan. Two million people were killed. The young girls were captured by them to be made slaves or wives, but they planned to kill all the young boys."

"We were told to flee. We had to leave right away with only the clothes on our backs and no provisions. There were over twenty thousand boys who fled. We faced danger on all sides. If we walked on the roads, the soldiers would shoot us down, so we had to go through the jungle. We were really scared because we knew there were poisonous snakes and all sorts of wild animals that could harm us. I was fourteen years old, but some were as young as six. Many boys were killed by lions during the journey. Some died of starvation or dehydration or became too weak to go on. We hiked over a thousand miles. We went through the desert, and the heat was terrible. I was so hungry and thirsty I didn't know if I was going to make it. Many of my friends walking beside me dropped dead. When we came to rivers, we had to swim across them. Crocodiles killed many of my people."

"First, we went to Ethiopia, where we stayed in a refugee camp. Then war broke out there, so we were forced to leave. We had to cross Sudan once again as we headed to Kenya. More boys were murdered by the occupying army. In the end, only about half of those who left Sudan with us made it to Kenya. We stayed in refugee camps in that nation for about nine years. I won a lottery to come to America. There were close to four thousand Sudanese youth who emigrated to the United States. We were sent to many different states. I went to Syracuse, New York, where I eventually graduated from college. I am currently looking for a job."

We realized now where we'd seen this young man before. He was one of *The Lost Boys of Sudan*, as the group is famously referred to. Several months earlier, we had watched a documentary on this story. He was in the film.

It was a blessing to meet Joseph. It's tragic that there is still a civil war in South Sudan. Over two and a half million people have fled the country; many are still staying in refugee camps.

CHAPTER EIGHTEEN

A Window of Opportunity

I was forced to take a window clerk position after working many years in the back of the post office sorting mail. I wanted nothing to do with this job, which was quite difficult with loads of pressure. I was often responsible for twenty thousand dollars a day, and the policy was that if your balance was off at the end of the shift, you were required to make up the difference from your own pocket. At least my accounting background finally became useful again.

But God had a plan in this uncomfortable switch. He revealed a whole new realm of ministry for me. You could say, it opened up a huge window of opportunity. In this section, I will be sharing the stories of some of the people I met through this position.

Desperate Souls

Ray came into the post office with a manila envelope to mail. We had gone to the same high school, so I immediately recognized him. He looked terribly troubled as he handed me the envelope. Something was obviously wrong, but naturally, I couldn't read his thoughts. I found out later that it was a suicide letter he'd sent to his family, and right after he left me, he killed himself. When I read his obituary in the newspaper, I was deeply disturbed. Could I have prevented it if I had just said something to him? I wondered.

Many years earlier, my oldest sister told me she didn't want to live any longer. I put my arms around her and tried to convince her that there was a purpose for her life. She was beautiful and only forty years old when she committed suicide. I was devastated along with the rest of the family. I don't think suicide victims realize how hard it is for those left behind. I don't think my parents ever fully recovered from my sister Renee's death. They carried the horrendous grief of that heart-wrenching trauma with them for the rest of their lives.

About a month after the first incident, another man came into the post office, who was horribly depressed.

"There's nothing left to live for!" he moaned. "I'm going home, and I'm going to shoot myself and end it all!"

I spoke up without hesitation. "That is not the answer! There is life after death and judgment!" I cried emphatically.

"What do you want me to do?" He responded pathetically.

"If I were you, I'd get down on my knees and cry out to God for help as soon as you get home!" I admonished him strongly. Fortunately, there were no other customers present during our intense dialogue. I believe that was God's mercy.

The next day this man came to me and fervently proclaimed, "That was the best advice anyone has ever given me! Thank you." I hadn't said anything profound, but it proves, at least in some cases, just a few words can save a life. "The Sovereign Lord has given a well-instructed tongue, to know the word that sustains the weary. He wakens me morning by morning, wakens my ear to listen like one being instructed" (Isaiah 50:4 NIV). I gave him a Bible and some inspirational books to read. He also visited our church the next week. A few years later, I officiated at the funeral of a dear friend, and this man was working at the funeral home. He approached me after the service and thanked me for giving him hope again.

Tragically, suicide has become an epidemic in our society. People think that they cannot escape their pain and feel like they're in a dark tunnel with no way out. They have lost all hope or purpose in life. They want relief from their suffering and come to believe that the only answer is suicide.

I would vehemently urge anyone in that condition to pour their heart out to God as my friend did since He is the only One who can give them the strength to cope with that kind of anguish. I would also advise them to find a good spiritual counselor to help with overcoming the trauma, which is causing their pain.

And I want to exhort anyone who suspects that they know a potential suicide victim to speak up and take action to help them.

Beverly and Allison

It was nice to see old friends occasionally while working at the window. One day I recognized a mother-daughter team who greeted me warmly. We'd gone to the same church years ago, and though I didn't know them well personally, I knew they were sincere believers and good people.

Beverly was in her early sixties. She was a kind and sensitive woman with an air of refinement. She had suffered through a difficult marriage for many years. Her husband, who had professed to be a Christian, had been unfaithful to her, and she had become divorced after twenty-five years of marriage.

Allison was in her early twenties, an attractive young woman, well-mannered, and mature for her years. They apparently had an exceptionally close relationship.

In our brief conversation, they let me know they were looking for a new church. They had visited several already but hadn't felt that they'd found the right fit. Did I have any ideas? I thought momentarily. They were quite conservative. I wasn't sure they would be comfortable in a spirit-filled denomination. But that seemed to be what the Lord put on my mind. So, I suggested they visit one particular church that I was familiar with. They agreed to try it.

Several weeks went by before I saw either of them again. One day, Allison came into the post office, smiling broadly. She said had she stopped by to thank me for recommending that church to them! I was grateful that they were so happy there. In fact, whenever she came to the post office for the next several months, she repeatedly thanked me for sending them to that congregation. Her mother was also effusive in praising me, but neither gave any details about their experience. *Wow,* I thought. *They must really be having a personal revival there. That pastor must be some kind of preacher!* It was always good to see Christians who were passionate about their faith.

I was more than a little surprised, then several months later, to find a wedding invitation in my mailbox. It was from Allison. She had become engaged to the pastor of that church, who was a young man about thirty years old. I had been an unintentional matchmaker!

Carol and I were honored to attend their wedding. And soon after that, we learned Beverly had also become engaged to a man who was a member of that church. The Lord certainly works in mysterious ways.

Elise

Elise's story is one of the most tragic tales I've ever heard. I met Elise and her two teenage daughters when I waited on them at the post office. She was an exceptionally friendly French woman who'd recently moved to the United States in search of a better life. She'd been through a divorce and some troubled times in France and was ready to make a fresh start here.

At first, she seemed ecstatic about her move. She was bubbling over with enthusiasm as she came to pick up her mail and send letters to family and friends. This phase lasted almost six months. She was always cheerful and talkative about her plans for her new life in

America. She only winced mildly when I tried out some of my high school French phrases on her.

Then one day, Elise came into the post office looking utterly distraught. She literally burst into tears right at the window as I waited on her and began to bare her soul to me. I felt bad about cutting her off, but there was a long line of people behind her, and I couldn't afford to let her go on for a half-hour. So, I gave her our card and told her she should call my wife. And that's what she did.

While still in France, Elise had arranged to come and live with her cousin temporarily until she could buy a house and car and live independently. This cousin was married and, therefore, discussed the plan with her husband. He agreed to have Elise and her girls come and stay with them under one condition—that she would make him her power of attorney. She naively consented to his demand without fully comprehending the legal implications of this decision.

When she arrived, she had four hundred thousand dollars in her bank account, comprising all of her life savings and the sizeable inheritance she had received from her family. After she signed the papers designating the role of power of attorney to Leroy, her cousin's husband, she asked him to buy her a car and a house and to pay cash for both. He agreed to do so, and soon she had a moderately priced car and moved into a very modest home in a neighboring town. The house was probably only valued at around eighty thousand dollars since it was quite small, and real estate in this area is still relatively inexpensive compared to most of the country.

Elise was content with her new digs and embarked on a home improvement campaign. She told me she spent about fifteen thousand dollars fixing it up. She reasoned that she was in good shape financially since she had been fairly frugal in her spending. She knew she couldn't legally get a job for a while since she didn't have a green card yet. She had previously worked as a massage therapist and planned to set up her own business in the near future.

Everything seemed to be going extremely well until one day, she visited the bank and checked her account balance. I can't believe she didn't have a heart attack when she read the amount. There was only thirty-seven cents! Leroy had drained the account! Unbeknownst to her, he'd used her money to take his whole family to Europe along with buying expensive cars, boats, and other items and probably paying off his own home to boot.

Who could fathom the rage, the grief, and the fear that she felt? And she had nowhere to turn! But this wasn't the end of the horror story! Soon after this, she received an eviction notice from her landlord! (The landlord she never knew she had for the house she thought she owned!) And then what seemed to be the final blow, Leroy came and confiscated her car—that is the car she thought was hers but which he had put in his own name!

Could there possibly be anything more horrific than this? Unbelievably there was! She had also learned that in the several weeks they had stayed with her cousin, Leroy had raped both her underage daughters! I'm sure no words could describe the heartache and the anger she felt! I'm truly amazed that she didn't suffer a total breakdown. She had no other relatives in this country and few friends here. We did what we could do to help, mainly a lot of listening. And our church helped her as much as possible.

The police, on the other hand, did next to nothing to assist her. She was treated almost like a non-person since she was not a U.S. citizen. We found that she was walking endless miles to try to deal with her business and even to do grocery shopping, so my wife became her personal chauffeur for several months, driving her and her daughters everywhere they needed to go.

We watched and prayed as she dealt with her nightmare. At the end of many grievous months, there appeared a small ray of hope. I won't say there could be a simplistically happy ending to a story like this, but God is merciful, and Elise met and fell in love with a man who seemed to truly love her and had the means to provide a good life for her and the girls. They eventually got married and are doing very well together.

Not to get into sermonizing, but I've found that there are a lot of bleeding hearts out there these days who can't possibly comprehend how a loving God could send anyone to hell. I think they should hear this story about Leroy. Barring an absolutely miraculous repentance, does anyone think he should go to heaven? Or would anyone want to go to a heaven populated with guys like Leroy? Just some food for thought.

Miss Japan

Being friendly was part of my job as a window clerk, but for Christians, it's a Biblical command, so I tried to go the extra mile.

A young, foreign college student appeared at the head of the line one day, so I asked her where she was from.

"Japan," she answered.

"Do you miss Japan?" I queried. She paused for a moment, and then her face suddenly lit up, as she was certain she'd understood me. She quickly turned to her girlfriends behind her. "Hee, hee, hee," she giggled.

"He thinks I'm Miss Japan." I heard her say clearly in her broken English.

After that day, she always put on her biggest smile whenever she came into the post office. I never had the heart to correct her misinterpretation. I did invite her to our Bible study called *Tuesdays with Morey,* and she gladly accepted my invitation. She was leaving soon to go back to Japan, and we gave her a Study Bible to take with her.

"This book will help me remember how kind you were to me," she responded gratefully.

Death and Taxes

Bernie and his wife, Blanche, pulled up to my house in a brand-new Cadillac. They had heard about my income tax business and wanted me to file theirs for them. I'd had a tax business on the side for about ten years to supplement my income.

Bernie was a big talker, and I heard most of his life story as I briefly questioned him about their financial situation. I quickly realized with their very modest income and his big fancy car that something didn't add up.

Was this guy with the mob? No, I decided he wasn't smart enough for that. He was a loudmouth who couldn't keep any secrets. I soon got the car story as well. In fact, he couldn't wait to tell me, though I hadn't expressed my curiosity.

The tale he told me seemed awfully far-fetched, but as they say, truth is stranger than fiction.

"I was driving down a highway in Florida," he recalled as he drew a deep breath. I was right behind one of those armored trucks when, all of a sudden, the back door flew open, and all these bundles of cash came rolling out onto the road. There were hundreds of them! He was nearly feverish with the recollection. His eyes practically bulged out of his head as he continued to divulge his greed-driven action. I pulled over, along with several other cars, and we all grabbed as much as we could," he panted.

"What happened to the Brink's truck?" I queried. "They didn't know nothin' about it! They just kept speeding down the highway," He roared with laughter.

I then informed him, "I'm not only a tax preparer, but I'm also a minister." This revelation made him nervous, and he began to fidget in his chair, but I didn't preach at him. I did his taxes for several seasons before I closed the business.

A few years later, his wife approached me at the window of the post office. She told me Bernie was dying and that he wanted me to visit him. It seemed obvious that the man was terrified of death. He wanted me to baptize him.

I gave her Billy Graham's *Peace with God* tract to give to her husband and mandated that he read it before I would consent to baptize him.

A few days later, she came back to me, sounding cheerful. She told me Bernie now had total peace since he'd read the pamphlet. He had given his life to God and no longer feared death. In fact, she said there was no need for me to come now. He felt ready to meet his Maker. I was glad for him when I read his obituary the following week.

It seemed ironic that as I recalled Bernie's account of the spilled cash, I read about a strikingly similar incident that had just happened within the month involving another Brink's truck. $175,000 flew out of that vehicle. Authorities are asking for it to be returned.

Tough Customer

Occasionally I had to deal with some tough customers. Sometimes we don't realize that God is testing us in certain situations. One day while I was working the window at the post office, a lady came in and threw her package on the counter, demanding that I tape it up for her. I was trying to be nice by accommodating her since we were not supposed to tape packages for customers.

Then she said in an ungrateful tone, "I don't like the color of that tape!"

I was trying to exercise self-control at that point because everything in me wanted to tell her off for her rude behavior. She then started to laugh and said, "You're a pastor, right?" She informed me that she was just trying to see how I would react and asked me if she could visit our church.

Lights in the World

A pastor friend of ours once asked his congregation, "How many of you are involved in any community activities that are not church-related?"

He saw only one hand raised. He asked this woman what she was involved with. Big mistake—it was a weight loss program!

He sought to raise the question of how Christians can expect to reach the world if they never associate with anyone outside of the church. I believe this is an extremely valid point.

My wife and I got involved with Literacy Volunteers for a season and found that to be a wonderful way to reach out to new immigrants in the community.

Carol tutored a Buddhist woman from Thailand, who became our friend and eventually accepted Jesus as her savior. When I related this to my friend, whose son was a missionary in Thailand for over ten years, he told me, "My son hasn't seen one conversion yet." Very few Buddhists convert to Christianity compared to people from other religions.

We also tutored a couple of young boys who had just immigrated to this country from Syria. They were in high school at the time. We have stayed in touch with them and are gratified to see that they have become quite successful in their careers. One became a pharmacist, and the other is a computer programmer. We have enjoyed ministering to people from different cultures and have learned a lot from them.

CHAPTER NINETEEN

Africa

I had been interested in missions for some time and had read many books on missionaries. I was especially fascinated by the life of David Livingston and other stories about Africa. My friend, Joe, had already been a missionary for several years in the Caribbean. After I loaned him some books about Africa, he and his wife were drawn to go there and serve. They ended up spending fifteen years there.

After they had ministered for a few years in Kenya, they came home on furlough and stopped to see us. Joe strongly urged me to visit them in Africa upon their return. My spirit witnessed to the idea, but I wasn't sure if I could afford it. I prayed that night and told the Lord that if He supplied the finances, I would go. Amazingly, the very next day, I unexpectedly received a large check, which was enough to cover the trip. I was thrilled. Carol wasn't quite as enthusiastic about the plan, but she decided to accompany me rather than be left behind.

It was a sixteen-hour flight to Nairobi, where Joe was stationed. He had scheduled me to preach at many churches there, which was a real blessing since Africans are generally much more zealous in their faith than Americans are.

I prayed before going to speak, and as always, I tried to get God's direction on what to share. As I was preparing for one service, I heard God's voice say clearly, "Don't take your wallet!" It wasn't an audible voice but the still small voice of the Holy Spirit speaking to my heart.

The service went well. We were impressed by the exuberance of the praise and worship and the spiritual hunger of the congregation. Afterward, the pastor of the church took us to a large city park where monkeys were running all around, much like squirrels do here. I got reprimanded for feeding them, but we still had a good time. We decided to take a taxi home, and with our African friends close beside us, we hailed a cab. The cab pulled up alongside the group, and just as we were ready to get in, I was tackled from the side and felt a hand go deep inside my pocket where my wallet normally would have been. The mugger thought he was getting a big wad, and he did! A big wad of Kleenex! Thankfully, I had obeyed God's command not to take my wallet that day, Phew! What a mercy that was. I'm glad I serve a God who still speaks to His people.

Our missionary friend had some rather unusual challenges in dealing with tribal cultures in Kenya. One example was the practice of the dowry in planning a marriage.

Young men were still required by long-standing tradition to pay large sums of money to their bride's family before a wedding could take place. A typical dowry was around seven hundred dollars an exorbitant sum in that country. In fact, most prospective grooms were simply way too poor to afford these financial obligations. Unemployment was about 40 percent when we visited Nairobi. Because of this, many couples were opting to live together, creating a moral dilemma for the church. The missionaries were attempting to abolish the dowry practice.

Many Africans were barely feeding their families. In the slums we visited, the children were thrilled to get a slice of bread when we passed out several loaves to a group of them. And we did see a few distended bellies of youngsters who were obviously malnourished—a heartbreaking situation.

We also heard from parents there who bemoaned the fact that their children weren't in school due to the tuition requirement for even the elementary grade levels.

We wanted to help as much as we could, though our means were limited. One project we had heard about was an orphanage that a pastor was planning to start. Our missionary friends were also enthusiastic about aiding this proposal.

When we returned to the States, we sent this man a check for $100 to assist in building the children's home. When we got the canceled check back, we were horrified to find the amount on it had been changed. Someone had added a three before the $100, changing the figure to $3100! This was an awful shock. The bank there had cashed the check, but thankfully our bank gave us a refund. This reminds me of a story from my childhood.

When I was ten years old, I had a friend who was a pretty bad character. I was quite naive, and my buddy, Stuart, was able to lead me astray.

He received a gift certificate for three dollars from the local department store. In the sixties, this was a generous gift. But Stuart wasn't satisfied with the amount, and he pulled out a pen and added a one, making it thirty-one dollars on the gift certificate.

To say my friend had a criminal mind at the age of ten would be putting it mildly. He then tried to get me to do his dirty work for him. He wanted a new bowling ball and told me how easy it would be to pull it off. I wanted nothing to do with this scheme until he bribed me with some rare coins. What Jewish boy wouldn't be tempted by a bag of rare coins?

I recruited my younger brother to be my accomplice in this crime. We pulled it off and brought the bowling ball and a basketball home with us, which cost exactly thirty-one dollars. My friend never gave me the coins he had promised; instead, he handed me the basketball.

Stuart had commanded me, "Don't let them drill the holes in the bowling ball, or it won't fit my fingers." He later went back to the store claiming his brother gave him the ball so he could get it drilled. I had tremendous guilt for years over this incident.

Was it just a coincidence, do you think, those figures $31 and $3100? The Bible says we reap what we sow (Galatians 6:7), and Numbers 32:23 (NIV) says, "...your sin will find you out." What goes around, comes around?

Another interesting event we experienced in Africa was being invited to dinner at one man's house. A tiny elderly couple who looked like pygmies were there. They were pointing at us and laughing.

I asked the host, "Why are they laughing at us?"

He replied, "They've never seen white people before, and they think you look like twins!" I posed for a picture with them, and I looked like Andre, the Giant even though I'm only five foot eight.

CHAPTER TWENTY

Israel

For years I had dreamed of visiting the Holy Land. I was elated when that dream finally became a reality. I was amazed by the beauty of Israel and excited to walk where Jesus had walked.

We went on a tour with a Christian group and traveled around the country, visiting many famous sites. We had a baptism service at the Jordan River, which is very shallow and looks quite dirty. A woman from Pakistan (whose population is less than 2 percent Christian) approached me and asked me to baptize her ("Christianity in Pakistan" 2020). She was fearful of the water, but with our help, she accomplished her goal. It was quite an experience to be in the same river where Jesus was baptized.

This tour group had good taste in accommodations, and when we concluded the tour in Jerusalem, we stayed at the renowned King David Hotel for a couple of nights, which has a five-star rating. I was so overloaded with luggage when we arrived that I put all three of my hats I'd brought with me on my head to free up my hands. Unfortunately, when we got to our room, there were some issues. I had to go to the front desk to deal with the situation.

I thought the clerk was eyeing me strangely, as I approached her. Was that a slight smirk on her face as she met my gaze? I almost felt as if she was laughing at me, albeit silently. It seemed disrespectful, especially for such a swanky place. It was true that I wasn't accustomed to this level of luxury. Could the staff see that I didn't fit in?

After I explained the issues with the room, the desk clerk said, "We see that you have problems!" There was that smirk again! What snobbery! By then, I was sweating profusely, and suddenly my head seemed to be on fire! So, I took off my hat and then I took off a second hat and then a third! I broke down laughing when I realized how silly I'd looked, and the two desk clerks then joined in laughing heartily.

It was bad enough to make a fool of myself there once, but the next day I found myself in an even more ridiculous situation. I had gone to the pool for an early morning swim only to realize afterward that I had forgotten my room key.

My wife had already gone to the dining room for breakfast, and now I was locked out of my room. I could only think of one thing to do. I wrapped my towel over my bathing suit and headed for the dining room. Too bad I hadn't at least brought a shirt with me!

Tentatively, I entered the dining room in search of Carol and the room key. The head waiter immediately started screaming something at me in Hebrew. Quickly I was surrounded by a security team as everyone in the room turned to stare at me with shocked expressions! I think they thought I was a terrorist—a terrorist in a towel! So, I whipped off the towel as everyone gasped. When they saw my bathing suit, they all started laughing hilariously. The security guards just shook their heads and let me approach my wife. So, much for maintaining my dignity! After that, I just tried to stay in my room.

CHAPTER TWENTY-ONE

The Three Muslims

After a number of days, I finally heard from Mike the Turk. He explained that he had gone to New York City to visit some Muslim friends. Of course, there was nothing wrong with that, but when we visited him shortly after this trip, I sensed something had changed. He didn't seem too excited about the Turkish Bible that I had acquired for him. Furthermore, he said he wouldn't be able to go to church again since he'd agreed to help Nick on Sundays selling sunglasses.

Though I never learned the details, I think the Muslim friends he visited tried to turn him away from the Christian faith. They may have had good reasons to be sure! There's a high cost for Muslims who convert to Christianity in many countries. That cost can even be their lives.

Islamic tradition teaches that when Muslims leave the faith, the family members are to kill them! If they aren't put to death, they often lose their jobs and are shunned by friends and relatives. Another reason it's so hard for Muslims to convert to Christianity is that the Koran teaches them that they will go to hell if they believe that Jesus is God. I didn't hear from Mike for a few weeks after that visit, and I was concerned about his faith.

One day, as I was driving by a park, I saw the Turkish trio. I stopped to greet them, and they acted like I was their best friend. I learned that Mike would be returning to Turkey soon since he had completed his college course.

I was touched when he said, "I have many invitations from other friends, but I want to spend my last week with you."

I bought him an English Study Bible, and he was excited when he recognized the names of the seven churches in the Book of Revelation, which are all in Turkey. When he returned to his country, he emailed me and thanked me again for the Bible, and said he was continuing to study it.

Nick and I continued our friendship. I'm certainly willing to be friends with anyone whether or not they ever accept Christ, and I'm not going to pressure anyone to convert. Nick had told me from the beginning of our relationship that he wasn't at all interested in religion. This made it even more remarkable that he voluntarily came to our Bible study. He appeared to be a tough nut to crack spiritually, though.

One day, I felt the Lord speak to me to loan him the movie, Abraham. I was a little apprehensive as to what his response would be. I went to his house, but since he wasn't home, I left the video on his doorstep. I was surprised when he showed up at my home the next day. This film had genuinely moved him! It made such an impact on him that he wanted to watch all the other Bible videos I had. After he finished watching all of them, he started renting more from my friend, Dale, at the local Christian bookstore.

He had some interesting questions for me regarding one part of the Abraham story. He was curious to know why Abraham had set out to sacrifice Isaac instead of Ishmael because the Koran teaches that it was Ishmael he offered up to God. I believe seeds of faith were sown in his heart through our discussions. He also moved back to Turkey, but he visited the U.S. again the following year, bringing us gifts from his homeland.

It can be difficult for people from other cultures and religious backgrounds to feel accepted in our society. Christians are commanded to be lights in the world. We are specifically called to reach out to those the Bible calls "strangers". This would include all immigrants and visitors to our country. Immigrants bring the foreign mission field right to our doorstep. What could be a better opportunity for ministry?

CHAPTER TWENTY-TWO

Two More Muslims

My wife and I were visiting New York City. This was no small day trip from our tiny town in upstate New York—a good five hours each way, even with taking a train for about half of the journey.

As we looked for a restaurant there, we passed by a group of radical Muslims shouting to a crowd on the sidewalk. They were large men about the size of linemen on a football team, and they were seething with wrath. I could see the hostility in their eyes. I immediately decided this bunch would not be open to a Bible study.

"We don't want the god of Christianity! He's a sissy who forgives sinners! We want Allah, the god of Mohammed, who is a warrior!" The negative energy of their words was like a poisonous gas filling the air.

We were relieved to get inside the restaurant. I was starting to relax and look at a menu when the waiter came along, and my wife asked him if he was a Christian.

"No, I'm a Muslim," he politely responded. "We're Christians, and we would like to talk to you about Jesus," she boldly proclaimed. Oh boy, here we go again. I wasn't sure if this was wise after what we'd just witnessed outside. But as I've said, my wife tends to be prophetic and often sees opportunities before I do.

The waiter was laughing now. "Is Jesus going to come back as a baby again?" he quipped.

"He's coming back as the Lion of Judah," I replied. This led to a deep spiritual discussion. "Do you know what your eternal destiny will be?" I probed gently. According to the Koran, no one is promised to go to heaven unless they die a martyr. Even Mohammed confessed he couldn't be certain where he would go.

This young man then told us he wasn't a good Muslim because he couldn't keep the five pillars of Islam. The five religious requirements in life for a Muslim are: to recite the Shahada, the profession of their faith, pray five times a day, give alms to the poor, fast during the month of Ramadan, and make a pilgrimage to Mecca at least once in a lifetime.

Our server said he was working three jobs just to make ends meet and didn't think he'd ever be able to afford a trip to Mecca. We explained that salvation is a free gift in the Christian faith. He now seemed more receptive to what we were saying. Incredibly we must have talked for at least twenty minutes before his boss finally came around and demanded that he get back to work. It turned out to be a very positive experience for us, and like our three Turkish friends, this guy seemed to enjoy the discussion as well.

While we don't attempt to share our faith with everyone we meet, we try to hear from God's Spirit when and how to approach people.

Iranian Muslim

On our return trip from Israel, we had a real divine appointment. The Turkish airlines were a lot cheaper to fly, so we went that route. It was frustrating when we landed in Istanbul because no one seemed to speak English, and the airport was mass confusion. We finally boarded the airplane after full-body scans by security. I guess we looked suspicious!

We sat down and relaxed, waiting for takeoff. A black-haired man sat down next to me. I introduced myself and my wife to him and found out he was from Iran. He was traveling to the United States and seemed ecstatic to get out of his native land.

My wife was at it again! She whispered, "Why don't you give him a Bible study?"

"No way, he's a Muslim and probably not interested," I retorted.

He was talkative and friendly and soon asked us, "Is that a Bible on your seat?"

My wife nudged me, "Yes, would you like to hear a short Bible study?" I nervously responded.

"Well, I'm not a good Muslim, and I would like to learn about the Christian religion," he replied. Could God have made it any clearer? Carol was moving in the prophetic once again.

I opened to Psalm 34 and started sharing about how God looks at the heart attitude of man. You can never be good enough to earn your way to heaven. Salvation is a gift. "For it is by grace you have been saved, through faith and this is not from yourselves, it is the gift of God, so that no one can boast" (Ephesians 2:8–9 NIV). It was amazing how he responded and how open he was to the gospel. It seemed like we were talking for hours. He then told me, "When I arrive in the United States, I'm going to visit churches. I hope I can stay in your country."

God undoubtedly has a sense of humor using a Messianic Jew to witness to an Iranian Muslim. And what I found just as ironic was the fact that there were three Hasidic Jews sitting directly behind us. I turned around, and by the looks on their faces, they had heard every word I had said. Talk about getting an audience!

CHAPTER TWENTY-THREE

A Man Sent by God

For quite a few years, Carol and I had discussed the possibility of leaving the church. I had pastored for almost fifteen years when I felt God speaking to me that it was time to move on. One of our main concerns was the question of who would take over as pastor when I left since it was a small and exceptionally poor congregation that could not afford to offer a pastor's salary.

One Sunday, a man came to visit our church. He was new in town and had been looking for a place to worship. He was a mature believer and a man of prayer, so he asked God to lead him to the right church. He had walked around the heart of the city for several days stopping in front of quite a few big, old church buildings but had felt no witness or desire in his spirit to visit any of them. Then, he "just happened" to walk by the small storefront we were renting on Main St. and saw our sign. He instantly felt a warmth in his heart, knowing that this was the church God was leading him to.

James was a pastor from the Island of St. Vincent in the Caribbean. He and his family had initially moved to Brooklyn. Then his daughter bought a couple of houses at an auction in Gloversville with the goal of getting them away from the big city. What were the chances of our paths crossing? But the Scriptures say: "The steps of a good man are ordered by the Lord…" (Psalm 37:23 KJV).

James was a gifted worship leader, and he and his son, OJ, were both musicians, which was just what we needed in our congregation. They blessed us by teaching us many lively praise songs from their country. We had a Caribbean beat in our worship services! James soon demonstrated that he was anointed to preach, as well. And I appreciated that despite all of his abilities and talents that he invariably demonstrated a servant's heart and was always submissive to my authority as pastor.

I didn't have to search for a replacement. God had sent him to me, and he agreed to take over the church when I left. In fact, God did a marvelous work through James in merging our church with another small congregation in the community.

My wife and I have been doing quite a bit of traveling in the last few years and are preparing for more ministry in the future. We don't believe that total retirement is biblical.

We received a personal prophecy when we left the church that for us, "The best is yet to come!"

MORRIS AARON SHAPIRO

Epilogue

I believe that Christianity is the only way to God and that the Bible is God's inspired word. The Bible clearly states that Jesus is God.

John 1:1 (KJV) says,

> *In the beginning was the Word, and the Word was with God, and the Word was God.*
> *And the Word became flesh and dwelt among us.*
>
> (John 1:14 ESV)

> *The Son is the radiance of God's glory and the exact representation of His being.*
> (Hebrews 1:3 NIV)

This is a major stumbling block for many people. One question often posed is: What happens to those who have never heard the gospel?

Christians are commanded by God in Mark 16:15 (NIV) to "...Go into all the world and preach the gospel to all creation." Matthew 24:14 (NIV) says, "And this gospel of the kingdom will be preached in the whole world as a testimony to all nations, and then the end will come." God has given His people this assignment, but many Muslim and atheistic nations have closed their doors to missionaries.

We must remember that God has no limitations and will reach people who have a heart for Him. He is all-knowing, all-powerful, and His Spirit is present everywhere. He doesn't force anyone to choose Him, but He knows the thoughts of every person on earth and understands their hearts. He will search for anyone who will respond to Him.

Muslims today are converting to Christianity in record numbers, and 25 percent of those who have converted had dreams or visions where Jesus appeared to them (Klett 2019). 2 Chronicles 16:9 (NIV) says, "For the eyes of the Lord range throughout the earth to strengthen those whose hearts are fully committed to Him."

2 Peter 3:9 (NIV) says, "The Lord is not slow in keeping His promise, as some understand slowness. Instead, He is patient with you, not wanting anyone to perish, but everyone to come to repentance."

God's desire is for all humanity to spend eternity with Him in heaven. God is full of love, and He is just. He will give all of His creation an equal opportunity to choose Him.

I want everyone to experience the same joy and fulfillment that I've found in following Jesus. I encourage anyone who reads this book to pray and ask God to forgive your sins and to reveal Himself to your heart. You will never be the same again.

Appendix

A Comparison of Judaism, Islam, and Christianity

In comparing the religions of Judaism, Islam, and Christianity, we find quite a few similarities but also many differences. Each religion is based on its own holy book. These religions, like most others, have a great leader who is the founder and center of the faith. We will look briefly at the three belief systems, their leaders, and their sacred texts. In examining and presenting these religions, I am trying to present facts. I realize that not all who profess these faiths, take what's written in their holy books literally.

All three religions believe in a god who is sovereign, which means he possesses supreme or unlimited power. They also all believe their god has the absolute truth and that this truth is revealed in their holy books. All embrace the concept of a god who created the universe and revealed himself to humanity.

Each of these religions believes in an afterlife ending in either heaven or hell. They each believe in a judgment day when their god will determine the eternal destiny of all humanity. The holy books of each faith reveal the character of each religion, their god, and his requirement for eternal life.

Since I have a background in Judaism and Christianity, I was curious to learn what Muslims believe and desired to read and study the Koran. I was trying to understand why over a billion people profess to be of the Islamic faith. I was trying to be very open-minded and realized that nobody should be afraid of exploring other religious texts than your own.

I decided to read the Koran and a few biographies of Mohammed. According to Muslim beliefs, you can only read the Koran in Arabic to keep its purity. Translating it into common languages is prohibited. Since I read the Koran in English, this was unacceptable according to their beliefs. I also read several other books by expert Islamic scholars.

Very few Muslims can read Arabic, so they must trust imams (their religious leaders) to decipher its content for them. When we tutored the children who immigrated from Syria, they informed us, "We had three hours of religious training in school each day."

Mohammed called the Christian Old and New Testaments "the books," which he considered holy books, but according to Islam's teaching, they had become defiled and could no longer be trusted. Muslims believe that the Koran is the final authority.

When Mohammed was forty years old, as he was praying alone in a cave, he heard a voice speak to him. He wasn't sure at first whether this voice was from Allah (the Muslim god) or demonic in origin. His wife convinced him that Allah was speaking to him through the angel Gabriel. This voice told him to recite the words he heard. In the seventh century, almost all Arabs were illiterate, so all they could do was recite. For the next twenty years, he believed Gabriel spoke to him and told him to recite what he heard, so he wouldn't forget his instructions. Twenty years after his death, these words were recorded, establishing the Koran in the seventh century.

There are many stories in the Koran that are similar to those in the Old and New Testaments. Some believe many caravans passed through Mecca, and Mohammed heard many accounts from those of the Jewish and Christian faiths incorporating them into his doctrine. But some of the Koran contradicts the biblical accounts. For example, in the Koran, Noah had four sons, not three, and Abraham prepared to sacrifice Ishmael instead of Isaac. Jesus is considered solely a prophet, not the Son of God. Muslims also don't believe that it was Jesus crucified on the cross, but someone who looked like him. Interestingly, the Koran was written over six hundred years after Jesus' crucifixion. I can't believe that it wasn't Jesus on the cross because of historical evidence and eyewitnesses who wrote about it in the first century.

Another problem I discovered while reading the Islamic verses was contradictions within the Koran itself. If something is inspired by God, why would He change it? According to Muslim scholars, the last messages from Allah to Mohammed would cancel out the first if there are contradictions. For example, in the earliest parts of the Koran, it promotes an attitude of respect for Jews and Christians, but in later surahs or chapters, it advocates violence against them, which is considered the last message from Gabriel to Mohammed.

There are also many other disturbing and violent verses in the Koran—over one hundred that speak of war with non-believers. Some are quite graphic with commands to chop off heads and fingers and to kill infidels wherever they may be hiding.

Jesus, who is a revered prophet to Muslims, gave instructions on discerning false prophets. He said, "You shall know them by their fruits..." (Matthew 7:16 KJV).

This refers to their character. We will briefly examine the lives of Mohammed, Moses, and Jesus to determine their characters.

Mohammed claimed he was the last and greatest prophet of God. The Koran only mentions Mohammed four times and tells little of his life. The Hadith, another holy book of the Islamic faith, goes into great detail about Mohammad's life.

According to the Koran, Muslim men are allowed to have four wives at one time. Mohammad had twenty wives in his lifetime, and he had nine at one time. He even had a wife who was only a nine-year-old child when he married her.

At first, Muslims only used violence to defend themselves; however, in Mohammed's later years, they began to attack and destroy the villages of those they considered infidels. They gave their captives three choices if they wanted to live: convert to Islam, pay a tax, or flee. A Muslim in Syria was observing the behavior of ISIS there recently, and after reading the Koran for himself, he concluded, "ISIS is the Koran!" He found that they were literally doing what the Koran said to do. I realize that most Muslims don't practice violence or necessarily condone these violent verses. The problem is that their reference point, the Koran, advocates these very disturbing practices.

A good book to read on this subject is *Seeking Allah, Finding Jesus* by Nabeel Qureshi. It describes how a devout Muslim converted to the Christian faith.

As I mentioned previously, the requirements of the Islamic religion are: to recite the Shahada the confession of their faith, pray five times a day, give alms to the poor, fast for the month of Ramadan, and once in a lifetime to make a pilgrimage to Mecca. These are the five pillars of the faith. Islam teaches that each person has two angels recording their good and bad deeds, which will determine their eternal destiny. No one can know for certain if they will go to heaven or hell. The only way a person of this faith can be guaranteed to go to heaven is by dying a martyr in a holy war or jihad.

The ultimate belief of the Islamic religion is that they are the one true religion. As long as you submit to Allah and his messenger Mohammed, there is peace.

The two main sects of Islam are Sunni and Shiite. Their differences arose over the question of who would succeed Mohammad after his death. The Shiites believe that all successors must be direct descendants of Muhammad's family (Melina 2011). About 75 percent of the Muslim population are Sunni (Melina 2011). The Sunnis believe that Mohammad had no rightful heir and that his successors should be elected by the religious community (Melina 2011). Another difference between the major branches of Islam are their beliefs regarding the Mahdi, which is Arabic for the guided one. This character is a type of redeemer in the Islamic faith. The Sunnis believe he has not been born yet. The Shiites believe he was born in 869 A.D. and will return to earth under Allah's orders.

Many believe that Muslims worship the same god as Christians and Jews do. This is not true. Allah is not a personal god like the God of Judaism and Christianity. He cannot be known according to Islam. Muslims tend to believe that everything that happens is Allah's will. The Koran is their ultimate authority. I remember talking to a Lebanese Muslim who had lost some relatives in the Virginia Tech shooting. He said, "It was Allah's will that it happened." I replied, "I believe man has free will, and that's why it occurred." God is sovereign and can choose to do whatever He desires, but I believe He is a God of love.

Judaism

Judaism is the oldest monotheistic religion in the world, which is a religion that believes there is only one God. There are three major branches of Judaism: Orthodox, Conservative, and Reform. The Orthodox interpret the scriptures very literally, while the Conservatives are more moderate, and the Reform are more liberal in their interpretation of scripture. The writings in the Hebrew scriptures are their reference point. The first five books of the Jewish scriptures, called the Torah, tell the story of God's creation of the world and reveal His plan and purpose for humanity. These five books are also the beginning of the Christian Bible.

God created man in His own image and gave him dominion over all the earth (Genesis 1:26). God desired a close personal relationship with humanity. This is illustrated by the way He walked and talked with Adam in the Garden of Eden (Genesis 3:8).

God tested Adam and Eve's obedience, and they gave into temptation and disobeyed His command. As a result, man's relationship with God was greatly damaged. Sin separates man from God because God is holy and can't have fellowship with anyone yielding to sin. Thankfully, God created a plan to redeem humanity, which is revealed in the Jewish scriptures.

God, in His redemptive plan, spoke to many Jewish prophets, Noah, Abraham, and Moses, to name a few. God spoke to Moses when He inspired him to write the books of the Torah. The Jewish religion is based on many scriptural laws, especially the Ten Commandments. Moses is revered in the Jewish faith and called one of the greatest prophets.

Moses had a fascinating life, which is described in the book of Exodus. Moses was called to be the deliverer of Israel. The pharaoh of Egypt had ordered that all the male Hebrew babies be killed. Moses' mother hid him in a basket, which she placed in the Nile, and he was found by the pharaoh's daughter and adopted by her. During the first forty years of his life, he was educated in all the ways of the Egyptians. He was being groomed to be the next pharaoh of Egypt when he discovered his Jewish roots.

The Israelites were slaves to the Egyptians for four hundred and thirty years. Moses saw the oppression his people were going through, and in a rage, killed an Egyptian. He had been called to be the deliverer of Israel, but he didn't wait for God's timing and direction. He now had to flee into the wilderness because of his act of murder.

He spent the next forty years in the wilderness, not realizing that God was preparing him to deliver His people from the tyranny of Pharaoh. The Scriptures teach that God's people must learn humility and come to understand His goodness. Moses became the meekest man on the face of the earth during his forty years in the wilderness (Numbers 12:3). His character was tested by God, and he succeeded in overcoming his pride and arrogance, though it took many years. When God tests us, we must trust in His faithfulness to help us overcome our problems.

In Exodus chapter 3, God spoke to him in a burning bush about delivering His people. Because of his humility, God spoke to him face to face (Exodus 33:11). Moses asked God to show him His glory, and He did in Exodus 34:6 (NLT), "The LORD passed in front of Moses, calling out, 'Yahweh! The LORD! The God of compassion and mercy! I am slow to anger and filled with unfailing love and faithfulness.'"

Moses received the Ten Commandments on Mt Sinai, which were God's laws that He wrote on two stone tablets. These laws give us specific instructions on how to honor God, our parents, and our neighbors, meaning all humanity. The Jewish rabbis wrote 613 rules on how to specifically follow these commandments. They are all really fulfilled in the two great commandments in the books of Deuteronomy and Leviticus, "You shall love the LORD your God with all your heart, with all your soul, and with all your strength" and "love your neighbor as yourself" (Deuteronomy 6:5 NKJV; Leviticus 19:18 NIV).

The Jewish people believe when they face God on judgment day, they will be judged according to the law. Daniel 12:2 (NIV) says, "Multitudes who sleep in the dust of the earth will awake: some to everlasting life, others to shame and everlasting contempt."

Since man continually sinned and broke His ordinances, God made a provision for man's sins, by commanding the sacrifice of animals. Their blood atoned for the people's sins.

There were specific instructions for these sacrifices, and certain times they were to be followed. Two of the most important times were the Day of Atonement (Yom Kippur), when the high priest went into The Holy of Holies, the special area of the temple where God dwelt to offer sacrifices for man's sin once a year. The Israelites were commanded to celebrate Passover every year to remember how God set them free from slavery to the Egyptians.

There are also many prophecies in the Old Testament about a Messiah who would deliver the Jewish people from oppression. In fact, there are over three hundred prophecies depicting two types of Messiahs, a suffering one and a kingly one. Most of the Jewish people are still waiting for their Messiah to appear, but some, like myself, believe He has already come—that Jesus is the Messiah. We are called Messianic Jews.

Yitzhak Kaduri was a famous rabbi who lived in Israel. He died in 2006 when he was one hundred eight years old, and over one hundred thousand people paid him respect at his funeral.

He claimed that God had revealed the identity of the Messiah to him. He wouldn't tell anyone what he had heard, but he wrote the revelation down and put it in a sealed envelope. He ordered that the envelope not be opened until one year after his death. When it was opened by his family members in front of their synagogue, they were flabbergasted because of the name he wrote on the paper: Yeshua, the Hebrew name for Jesus.

Unfortunately, many have closed minds, and despite the hundreds of prophecies Christ fulfilled at His first coming, most Jews reject Him as the Messiah. Jesus promised to come back and restore Israel, which would fulfill the kingly prophecies.

I really believe that Christianity is the completion of the Jewish religion. Jesus and all His followers were Jewish. Jesus said, "Do not think that I came to destroy the Law or the Prophets. I did not come to destroy but to fulfill" (Matthew 5:17 NKJV).

There are some problematic verses and stories in the Old Testament. Some behaviors of kings are also difficult to understand. King David had eight wives and committed adultery. God obviously did not approve of his actions. He paid a grievous penalty for his affair with Bathsheba and did repent when he was confronted by the prophet Nathan regarding his sins (Psalm 51). Yet, despite his serious transgressions, David is called a man after God's own heart (Acts 13:22). This is illustrated in Psalm 51, where David writes a beautiful prayer of repentance. Though he had serious issues, he loved God wholeheartedly and desired to have an intimate relationship with his Creator, which was always God's plan for His people.

The recorded history in the Old Testament is very honest and doesn't justify man's sins. Israel was severely punished for her disobedience. We need to understand God's redemptive work and man's fallen nature to understand some of these accounts. In 1 Samuel 15, King Saul was ordered to kill all the Amalekites. God, in His foreknowledge, could see that the Amalekites would always oppose Israel.

God promised after the fall that He would redeem His people. A Messiah would have to be born from the seed of Judah, one of the twelve tribes of Israel. Any nation that would prevent the Messiah from being born would have to be dealt with. When King Saul disobeyed God and didn't destroy the Amalekite race, this led to near annihilation for Israel.

In the book of Esther, Haman petitioned the king (and almost succeeded) to destroy all of the Israelites.

Haman was an Amalekite. Queen Esther saved Israel when she revealed Haman's evil plot.

There is a continuous battle between God and Satan in the Bible. Ever since Satan was cast out of heaven, he has tried to thwart God's plans. He thought he had won in the garden of Eden by causing Adam and Eve to yield their authority to him, but he lost when Christ was crucified and resurrected from the dead. In order to understand Scripture, you must apprehend the whole picture.

Christianity

Christianity has its foundation in the Jewish scriptures, which make up the Old Testament of the Bible. The Bible is made up of the Old and New Testaments. Christians believe both these testaments were inspired by God (2 Timothy 3:16). There are sixty-six books in the Bible. It contains thirty-nine books in the Old Testament and twenty-seven in the New Testament.

The main focus of the New Testament is the life of Jesus Christ, who claimed to be the promised Messiah and God in the flesh (John 14:9). He fulfilled all the requirements of the Old Testament and established a New Covenant or Testament in which His followers are no longer judged by the law but are now justified by faith.

Christianity reveals an epic love story between God and man. God was willing to sacrifice His only son to redeem humanity. The first man, Adam, failed. Therefore Christ, who is called the second Adam, had to defeat Satan as a man. Christ, who was God in human form, had to leave heaven and come to the earth limited as a man to save the world from Satan's destruction.

We must go back to Genesis to fully comprehend this magnificent story. God said, "Let Us make man in Our image, according to Our likeness: let them have dominion over all the earth..." (Genesis 1:26 NKJV). Man was given free will allowing him to choose good or evil.

God then put Adam in the Garden of Eden to guard it and keep it (Genesis 2:15). "And the Lord God commanded the man saying, 'Of every tree of the garden you may freely eat: but of the tree of the knowledge of good and evil you shall not eat, for in the day you eat of it you shall surely die'" (Genesis 2:16–17 NKJV). Satan, in the form of a serpent, tempted Eve while Adam watched. When they chose to disobey God and listen to Satan by eating from the forbidden tree, it created a tremendous barrier in their relationship with God. Man's choice to be independent of God brought catastrophic results.

Man became separated from God and now had a sinful nature, which all humankind would inherit from

Adam. He experienced fear, shame, and guilt for the first time in his life. Man also became self-centered instead of God-centered. Because of man's disobedience to God, Satan gained authority over the whole world, and the results have been chaos and destruction. 2 Corinthians 4:4 (NLT) says, "Satan who is the god of this world has blinded the minds of those who don't believe..."

Jesus, the second Adam, had to defeat Satan as a man without sin until the day He was crucified. Jesus was led by God's Spirit into the wilderness to be tempted by Satan. The Devil tempted Him in the three major areas of mankind's weakness: in the lust of the flesh, the lust of the eyes, and the pride of life (1 John 2:16). Jesus defeated the Devil in all these areas by using "the sword of the Spirit," which is the Word of God, the Bible.

His final temptation came in the Garden of Gethsemane where He struggled with going to the cross, but He prayed, "Father, if you are willing, take this cup from me; yet not my will, but yours be done" (Luke 22:42 NIV).

Hebrews 4:14–15 (NIV) says, "Therefore, since we have a great high priest who has ascended into heaven, Jesus the Son of God, let us hold firmly to the faith we profess. For we do not have a high priest who is unable to empathize with our weaknesses, but we have one who has been tempted in every way, just as we are—yet He did not sin."

Jesus died on the cross in our place as the fulfillment of the Passover lamb in Exodus 12:5, and His shed blood paid the price for all our sins. "For He made Him who knew no sin to be sin for us, that we might become the righteousness of God in Him" (2 Corinthians 5:21 NKJV). Christ paid the price to redeem all humanity, but each person must choose to receive Him into his or her heart to be forgiven. Isaiah 53:3–7 (KJV), was written hundreds of years before Christ's great sacrifice on the cross,

He is despised and rejected by men, a man of sorrows, and acquainted with grief: and we hid as it were our faces from him; he was despised, and we esteemed him not. Surely he hath borne our griefs and carried our sorrows, yet we did esteem Him stricken, smitten of God, and afflicted. But He was wounded for our transgressions, He was bruised for our iniquities: the chastisement for our peace was upon him, and with his stripes we are healed. All we like sheep have gone astray, we have turned every one to his own way; and the Lord hath laid on him the iniquity of us all. He was oppressed and he was afflicted, yet he opened not his mouth: He is bought as a lamb to the slaughter, And as sheep before its shearers is dumb, so he opened not his mouth.

Jesus Christ became the final Passover lamb (1 Corinthians 5:7). This was the crucial defeat of Satan when Jesus restored man to God by His death, burial, and resurrection. He had broken the curse of death by His resurrection, but the price was heavy.

John 3:16 (KJV) declares, "For God so loved the world, that he gave his only begotten Son, that whosoever believeth in him should not perish, but have everlasting life."

Some say this sounds like a fairy tale. The difference is that it is based on historical facts and hundreds of prophecies that have been fulfilled. Many atheists have turned to Christ after examining all the evidence for Jesus' resurrection. Lee Strobel, the author of *The Case for Christ* and Josh McDowell, who wrote *Evidence That Demands a Verdict*, are two noteworthy examples.

I took a course at the university, which I enjoyed, called New Testament Archeology. It taught me just how incredibly accurate the Bible is. My professor was an extraordinarily learned man who knew nine languages and had written our textbook. He had been on many archaeological digs, which had produced verification for scriptural content.

This professor stated, "Every geographical location mentioned in the New Testament has been found, and every account about kings and leaders has been proven accurate."

The discovery of the Dead Sea Scrolls has virtually verified the authenticity of the whole Old Testament. Every book is included in the scrolls except for the Book of Esther. These scrolls, which are dated hundreds of years before Christ, also verify all the Messianic prophecies.

A man once offered any person who could fulfill all these prophecies one hundred thousand dollars. But no one can control where they're born or the manner of their birth, much less the circumstances surrounding their death and burial, which are specific prophecies mentioned about the Messiah. It's astounding to realize that there are over three hundred prophecies, which are all extremely accurate. Psalm 22 and Isaiah 53 both give a detailed description of the crucifixion.

All who want to disprove Christianity must come to grips with the resurrection of Jesus Christ. Most historians will say that the four Gospels: Matthew, Mark, Luke, and John, are considered historically accurate because they were written shortly after His death. All four accounts describe the resurrection of Christ from the dead and the effect it had on all His disciples. The tomb was empty. If the Romans or the Jews could have produced the body of Jesus, which they desperately wanted to do, there would be no Christianity.

The Jewish leaders demanded that the Romans guard the tomb because they said (referring to Jesus) when that deceiver was alive, he said in three days I will arise (Matthew 27:63). Jesus predicted His own resurrection and fulfilled it.

Jesus' disciples all claimed to be eyewitnesses of His resurrection, and their transformation was astounding. They had all abandoned Him before the crucifixion except John. They were cowards. But when they saw Jesus after He rose from the dead, they became bold as lions even to the point of martyrdom. The Bible says in 1 Corinthians 15:5 that over 500 people witnessed Christ's resurrection, including His brother James. The Apostle Paul, who was once His enemy, also saw the risen Savior at a later time.

Christ's resurrection changed the course of history, and nothing could stop the spreading of Christianity, not persecution or even the threat of death in the Colosseum. Jesus said, "I am the resurrection and the life. He who believes in me, though he may die, he shall live.

And whoever lives and believes in Me shall never die..." (John 11:25 NKJV).

There have been many historic events that reflect a negative testimony about Christianity: The Crusades, the Spanish Inquisition, and the wars between Protestants and Catholics, to name a few. Those who were responsible for these atrocities thought they were promoting God's Kingdom on earth but instead were following the dictates of Satan.

None of these actions were supported by the teachings of the New testament. Jesus said, "...Love your enemies, bless them that curse you, do good to them that hate you, and pray for them which despitefully use you, and persecute you" (Matthew 5:44 KJV).

Christ is called the Prince of Peace and has always tried to win men with love, not by force. *The Sermon on the Mount* found in the book of Matthew, chapters five through seven, teaches us how to represent Christ on this earth. We're supposed to be lights shining in a very dark world.

Truth is ultimately decided by God, the Creator of the universe, not by man. Christianity reveals God's love for us. He demonstrated His love by sacrificing His Son for our redemption. Jesus said, "I am the way, and the truth and the life. No one comes to the Father except through Me" (John 14:6 NIV).

After examining all three religions with their holy books and the lives of the founders, I believe Christ is the Messiah and the answer to all man's needs. His life and character represent pure love.

C.S. Lewis said,

> A man who is merely a man and said the sort of things Jesus said would not be a great moral teacher. He would be a lunatic on the level of a man who says he is a poached egg— or else he would be the devil of hell. You must make your choice, either this man is the Son of God or else a madman or something worse. You can spit at him as a demon or you can fall at his feet and call him Lord and God.
>
> ("Quote by C.S. Lewis" n.d.)

References

Bala, R. 2017. *John Calvin - The Father of Reformed Theology*. CreateSpace Independent Publishing Platform.

Blair, Leonardo. 2020. "Woman Survives after Calling on Jesus When Husband Shoots Her, Then Kills Himself Outside Church." The Christian Post. 2020. https://www.christianpost.com/news/woman-survives-after-calling-on-jesus-when-husband-shoots-her-then-kills-himself-outside-church.html.

"Calvin's Reign of Terror." 2020. Three Eternal Destinies of Man. 2020. https://3eternaldestinies.org/calvins-reign-of-terror/.

Carmody, Bill. 2020. "3 Reasons Celebrating Your Many Accomplishments Is Critical to Your Success." Inc. Com 2020. https://www.inc.com/katie-burke/3-management-skills-most-leaders-lack-and-how-to-develop-them.html.

"Christianity in Pakistan." 2020. Wikipedia, The Free Encyclopedia. 2020. https://en.wikipedia.org/wiki/Christianity_in_Pakistan#cite_note-LoC-1.

Klett, Leah MarieAnn. 2019. "Muslim Who Sought to Kill Christian Cousin Embraces Faith after Jesus Appears in Dream." Christian Post. 2019. https://www.christianpost.com/news/muslim-who-sought-to-kill-christian-cousin-embraces-faith-after-jesus-appears-in-dream.html.

Lipka, Michael. 2015. "5 Facts about Catholicism in the Philippines." Fact Tank. Pewresearch. Org. 2015. https://www.pewresearch.org/fact-tank/2015/01/09/5-facts-about-catholicism-in-the-philippines/.

Melina, Remy. 2011. "What's the Difference Between Shiite and Sunni Muslims?" Live Science. 2011. https://www.livescience.com/33071-whats-the-difference-between-shiite-and-sunni-muslims.html.

"Quote by C.S. Lewis." n.d. Goodreads.Com. https://www.goodreads.com/quotes/6979-i-am-trying-here-to-prevent-anyone-saying-the-really.

The Holy Bible: English Standard Version [ESV]. 2007. Wheaton, Ill: Crossway Bibles. Public domain. https://www.biblegateway.com/versions/English-Standard-Version-ESV-Bible/#booklist.

The Holy Bible: King James Version [KJV]. 1999. New York, NY: American Bible Society. Public Domain.

The Holy Bible: New American Standard Bible [NASB]. 1995. The Lockman Foundation. http://www.lockman. org/nasb/index.php.

The Holy Bible: New International Version [NIV]. 1984. Grand Rapids: Zonderman Publishing House. https://www.biblegateway.com/versions/ New-International-Version-NIV-Bible/#booklist.

The Holy Bible: New Living Translation [NLT]. n.d. Carol Stream: Tyndale House Foundation. Tyndale House Publishers, Inc. https:// www.biblegateway.com/versions/ New-Living-Translation-NLT-Bible/#booklist.

The Holy Bible: The New King James Version [NKJV]. 1999. Nashville, TN: Thomas Nelson, Inc. https://www.biblegateway.com/versions/ New-King-James-Version-NKJV-Bible/#booklist.

"Vicious Flower Formulation." n.d. Psychology Tools. 2020. https://www.psychologytools.com/resource/ vicious-flower-formulation/.

Woldt, Hilary. 2017. "Forgiveness = Freedom." Milk and Honey Magazine. 2017. https:// milknhoneymagazine.com/forgiveness-freedom.

MORRIS AARON SHAPIRO

CPSIA information can be obtained
at www.ICGtesting.com
Printed in the USA
LVHW021531110820
662923LV00013B/1293